LETTING GO

A true story of
murder, loss and survival

BY RACHEL NICKELL'S SON
ALEX HANSCOMBE

HARPER
element

HarperElement
An imprint of HarperCollins*Publishers*
1 London Bridge Street
London SE1 9GF

www.harpercollins.co.uk

First published by HarperElement 2017

3 5 7 9 10 8 6 4 2

© Alex Hanscombe 2017

Alex Hanscombe asserts the moral right to
be identified as the author of this work

A catalogue record of this book is
available from the British Library

ISBN 978-0-00-814429-6

Printed and bound in Great Britain by
Clays Ltd, St Ives plc

MIX
Paper from
responsible sources
FSC™ C007454

FSC™ is   promote
the respon   rying the
FSC label   hey come
from   and

Fin   at

For those who seek the truth.

CONTENTS

FOREWORD

I do not claim to recollect all the events I have lived through with perfect objectivity or perfect clarity; indeed, it is true that we all see past events and experiences through the filters of our own beliefs and preconceptions. Even in hindsight, there is no such thing as twenty–twenty vision. Where appropriate, I have corroborated the details of events with those present so as to maintain the utmost accuracy and truth from start to finish.

In order to protect their identity, I have taken the liberty of changing the names of certain individuals concerned.

If the words of Shakespeare are true, and all the world is indeed a stage, then we have all played the roles of both hero and villain at different times. Therefore, it is with the understanding that people always act in the best way possible that I share this story with you.

PROLOGUE

'Alex, what was in the bag?'

I was the most famous child in the British Isles.

My third birthday had come and gone just days before and already I was on another scheduled visit to the child psychologist. As usual, the two detectives who had been assigned to us were both present.

Immediately after our last visit the psychologist's house had been fitted with hidden microphones and concealed cameras. The police didn't want to miss a word. While the purpose of these sessions was supposedly therapeutic, in reality their main objective was to obtain information. The killer had left nothing behind, and despite the hundreds of people on the Common that morning I had been the only witness. Only a footprint had been found during a forensic examination of the scene, along with a fleck of red paint in my hair.

Weeks had passed, the killer was still on the loose, free to strike again at any time. The police knew nothing about what took place in the minutes either before or after the attack. They were desperate for new leads and I was now the only person who could help them solve the puzzle they faced.

'I know how much you must remember your worst ever day,' the child psychologist began. 'The police are here to catch the bad man who killed your lovely mummy and to put him in prison where he won't be able to harm anyone else again.'

I was asked many questions that morning, questions I had already been asked many times and which were to be repeated over and again during the weeks to come. Usually I would spend the sessions playing with toys, and only address these strangers directly, if I addressed them at all, from time to time. But it was always clear to those present when the child psychologist intentionally took me back to relive the day in question that I was once again living in the moment the attack took place. My mind was totally focused and they couldn't help but imagine the film running in explicit detail inside my head.

'Alex, was the bad man carrying anything?' one of the detectives asked.

'A bag,' I replied.

'Alex, do you remember what colour the bag was?'

'Black.'

'Alex, what was in the bag?'

I played on for several seconds as the adults in the room looked at one another.

'Alex,' the detective repeated. 'Do you remember what was in the bag?'

Suddenly, I stabbed a crayon into the piece of paper on the table and gazed deeply into the detective's eyes, forcing him to lean forward to hear.

'A knife.'

CHAPTER 1

THE FIFTEENTH OF JULY

The southern wind
Doth play the trumpet to his purposes,
And by his hollow whistling in the leaves
Foretells a tempest and a blustering day.

Shakespeare, *Henry IV, Part 1*, Act V, Scene 1

Memories can be deceptive, seemingly playing tricks on us and reshaping our past perceptions in new ways. Some recollections fade over time, while others remain vividly etched into our memories. But in the depths of my mind there are still absolutes: the shelter and warmth of my mother's embrace, the knowledge that I was safe and that I was loved.

Of this I am convinced; when a seismic event changes the course of our lives, its impressions are marked on us forever, and the day I watched my mother's soul leave her body, on the morning of Wednesday, 15 July 1992, is one I will never forget. Twenty-four years have passed, but through the fog of time I can still see the film running inside my mind as if it were only yesterday.

For me, that morning began just like any other. I was less than a month away from my third birthday and I awoke in my small bed on one side of my parents' room, stretched out on the furry sheepskin on which I had slept since I was born.

I opened my eyes to see my mother gazing down at me from above. 'Good morning, Alex,' she exclaimed, lifting me up into her arms for a hug. I felt, as I had every day of my short life until then, a warm, happy feeling that began inside my chest and spread throughout my entire body; a feeling of lightness and peace.

While my mother went into the kitchen to prepare breakfast, my father picked me up and threw me onto their bed. I loved a good play fight with him. The two of us rolled on the covers together, wrestling and tussling until, after a couple of minutes, he got up, laughing, and said, 'OK, tough guy – time's up!'

Like most three-year-olds, I was full of energy and curiosity. I couldn't wait to start the day, and I was thrilled when our dog Molly – a sleek, seal-like bundle of shiny black fur with a furiously wagging tail – bounded into the room to say hello. A mixture of Labrador and greyhound, less than a year old and full of life and playfulness, she was my constant companion and like a younger sister. Not for the first time I wish she could have slept on my bed. She'd been allowed to do so the previous Easter, on holiday in the Isle of Wight. We were both delighted about it, but back at home there were strict rules to follow and Molly had to go back to sleeping on her bed in the kitchen.

Our apartment in Balham, South London, a two-bedroom flat on the third floor of a mansion block, was for now our sanctuary, a home where the three of us were shielded from the busy city beyond its walls. It was here where I was born and here I had spent all but a few nights of my young life.

I normally had breakfast in the front room, but that morning for some reason everything felt slightly different. Upon her return, my mother sat down on the bed beside me, handing me my bowl of cereal.

'If you're still hungry afterwards, you can have some toast and Marmite.'

She smiled at me as I dug into my cereal.

At the other end of the room, my father was pulling on the leather trousers he wore for work. He had usually left by the time I ate my breakfast, but that morning he was still at home and in a hurry. The evening before he'd been playing in a tennis tournament and he'd got back late.

Until recently he'd been travelling the globe playing tennis, but shortly before my birth he'd begun working as a motorbike dispatch rider. He was now working long hours, winding his way through endless city traffic, delivering parcels and packages. He worked hard to support the three of us, but my parents dreamed of making a new start. One day soon, they said, the three of us would travel together to the South of France and settle down in a small cottage in the depths of the countryside. Somewhere the sun shone every day; somewhere I could run wild with my hoped-for brothers and sisters; where the daily turmoil of city life would just be a thing of the past. But their plans were on hold until we could sell the flat.

As I finished my cereal my father bent down to kiss me and ruffle my hair. 'See you later, Alex. Have fun!' he said, before hugging my mother and kissing her goodbye.

'Bye, Daddy.' I smiled up at him as he opened the front door. I often had a bittersweet feeling watching him leave for work. By the time he got home I'd usually be asleep. But if I was still awake he would look at the drawings I'd done that day, listen to stories of our adventures with Molly and tuck me into bed, singing me a soft, soulful ballad until I drifted off into sleep. I loved these moments and felt sad knowing that I wouldn't be with him that day. But at the same time the long hours my mother and I spent together, just the two of us, were special.

Years later my father told me that although he very rarely missed work, that morning he felt a strong urge to stay at home.

After a disturbed night, during which I awoke several times, my mother had said to him, 'I'm so tired. I just want to sleep forever.' After all, she was always the one who got up and settled me back to sleep. Sometimes I would fall asleep again within seconds as she stroked my hair; while other times she would lift me up into her arms and cradle me tenderly, breast-feeding me until I drifted off once again.

Perhaps it was because she had been unusually subdued since her handbag was stolen from our car. It had been two days before when we went for our usual morning walk while my father was at work, and she'd left it in the glove box and forgotten to turn on the car alarm. When we returned to the car the window was broken, and the incident left her badly shaken.

As my father headed out the door, Molly began to bounce around the house, playing with her ball and getting under our feet. 'Come on, Alex,' my mother said, shaking off her low spirits. 'It's a lovely day. Let's get out for our walk.'

My mother and I spent every day together. At 23 she was truly beautiful – tall and athletic with long, golden hair and a smile that lit up her face. When I remember my mother, though, it's not in details like these, but the feeling of being loved and of loving in return.

While my father battled with the London traffic, our days always began with a walk. My parents liked to joke between them that I was like a puppy myself; both Molly and I needed long walks, so rain or shine my mother would take us to open spaces in an attempt to wear us out.

As I pulled on my shoes I looked hopefully at my yellow tricycle, parked in the hall. It had a long handle at the back that my mother could hold, to stop me pedalling headlong into the nearest road, and I loved it. I hoped that after our walk she might take me out on it.

Money was tight for my parents but my mother always filled our days with adventure. Every week she took me to the local library to choose books and at home we would make collages with patterns of pasta stuck on paper, put puzzles together on the floor and build castles and towers with building bricks piled up one on top of the other. Other times we played imaginary games together: I was always Babar, King of the Elephants, and she was always Celeste, my queen – the characters in one of the stories we liked to read best.

Minutes later, with our shoes firmly laced, we headed down the stairs to the street, holding each other's hand and grabbing on to Molly's lead with the other.

When we stepped out of the building my father was still there, wheeling his large, black motorcycle from the forecourt onto the street. As he pressed the starter and the engine roared into life, my mother and I stood together on the step waving goodbye to him. I was always excited by the loud roar of his bike, and loved watching him fire it up. He revved the engine fiercely one more time and I gave him a big smile before the sound of the exhaust pipes faded as he rode off into the distance. I did not know then that the next time I saw him our lives would be irrevocably changed.

My memories of that morning fast forward and I find myself walking beside my mother beneath the open blue skies of Wimbledon Common, the midsummer sun warm on our skin while Molly runs in circles around us, intoxicated by the sounds and smells of the park. I know of course that we had driven the twenty minutes across South London in our old grey Volvo, but details of the journey have long since faded away.

Until only a few weeks before we had regularly visited a local park near our home, but one morning a stranger exposed himself to my mother and we had not returned since. Wimbledon Common was in a wealthier area and both my parents felt it was a safer place for us to walk. My father had spent a great deal of his free time there as a child, running wild with his friends, and knew every inch of it by heart.

To me, the Common was a wilderness that stretched on forever; an untamed forest with endless leafy tunnels to explore and wide open spaces where Molly and the many other dogs that were brought there could run freely alongside picnicking families that sat together basking in the warm summer sun. Even in winter there were always people walking on the Common, and when temperatures dropped there was a large pond where parents, children and teenagers came to skate happily together.

As my mother and I walked hand in hand along a familiar path, we passed a spot I remembered well. It was here, in a quiet corner just off the path, that we had laid Birdie's body to rest only a few weeks before.

Birdie had entered our lives as my parents and I made our way back home from one of our weekend walks. Just outside the front door to our block of flats we spotted a beautiful bird lying on the pavement. Molly sniffed curiously while my parents crouched over it in concern and I watched, intrigued. The bird's wing was broken and none of us wanted to leave it there, so we decided to mount a rescue and my father quickly disappeared upstairs to find a cardboard box.

When he came back he lifted the bird gently into the box and carried it upstairs as my mother and I followed closely behind. In the living room he placed it on the floor and I peered into it, fascinated by the beady eyes which stared back at me. It wasn't long before we came up with the not so original name of 'Birdie', and for the next hour my father and I scratched around in the earth in the communal back garden, digging up worms, insects and other treats for Birdie, which we carried carefully back upstairs and attempted to feed to him with a pair of tweezers.

The next morning I woke to a loud burst of birdsong. Fascinated, I went running to look inside the box. Our devotion to Birdie was paying off – he was full of life and showing definite signs of recovery.

For a couple of days he continued to thrive. But when we came back from our walk one afternoon, Birdie was lying stiff and silent at the bottom of his box.

'What's happened to Birdie?' I asked.

'He doesn't need his body any more,' my mother explained gently. 'The part that's really him has gone somewhere else now.'

I listened thoughtfully as I studied his lifeless body.

A few days later we went to Wimbledon Common and chose a special place where we dug a shallow hole in the soil and gently laid Birdie's body to rest.

Soon afterwards my mother took me to our local library to pick out several children's books dealing with the subject. Over the next few days we read the books together and she explained to me that, even though I would perhaps be sad that Birdie had gone, he was now free and his broken wing was not hurting him any longer. He had gone to a beautiful place, where he could be happy.

'We are not our bodies,' she explained. 'The body is only like clothes that cover us for a little while.'

Less than a week before, we had been to a video shop and picked out a dinosaur cartoon for me to watch. It was called *The Land before Time*. When we got home I sat at my little red table, eating a sandwich and totally absorbed while my parents sat on the sofa behind me. In the film, a baby dinosaur, Littlefoot, was separated from his mother by a devastating earthquake. When he finally found her again she was lying weak and frail, collapsed on the ground, dying. The baby dinosaur nuzzled her as he pleaded desperately, 'Please get up! Get up!' But as much as his mother tried, she simply couldn't. She told him to carry on to the Great Valley and promised that she would be with him always, even if he couldn't see her.

I was glued to the screen as I watched the scene unfold. But to my father the thought of me – so devoted to my mother –

ever losing her in some kind of accident was too much for him even to contemplate.

'Switch it off,' he exclaimed, only half-joking. 'I can't take it!'

As the film played on I continued to watch wordlessly, keeping any thoughts I might have had to myself.

That warm July morning, as my mother and I walked past the place where Birdie was buried, we didn't stop. There was no reason. My mother had already explained to me that Birdie wasn't really there. He was now in a place of greater beauty and freedom – and what was once his body would now blend into the earth in order to create new life and repeat an infinite cycle.

Hand in hand we made our way down to the pond and headed back up the hill again, Molly trotting close by all the while. Soon we reached a large tunnel of trees, where sunlight appeared only dimly through the canopy above.

Nearby, a small stream wound through the woodland and the sounds of other parents and children laughing and calling to one another began to fade into the distance, replaced by the gentle splash of the stream. It had rained heavily in the previous few days; the grass was still wet and the air fresh.

As Molly headed into the bushes, following yet another tantalising trail, my mother and I carried on down the path. It was dark there, but as I looked up through the leaves I could see the blue of the sky beyond.

All of a sudden, as if sensing something was wrong, we both turned our heads to the right. Out of nowhere, a man with a black bag over his shoulder came lurching towards us through the undergrowth. There was no time to respond. I was grabbed and thrown roughly to the ground and my face forced into the mud. Seconds later my mother collapsed next to me. There were no screams. Everything was silent – so silent that for years to come the memories of those moments were to play out in my mind like an old film, without sound.

I saw the stranger's blank face, the clothes he wore and the knife he took from his bag. All these images remained so vividly engraved in my mind that later I would remember every single detail about him.

I picked myself up from the ground as fast as I could. I felt unsteady and my face was hurting. As I struggled to regain my balance, I caught sight of the man a few yards away, kneeling to wash his hands in the stream. A moment later he rose suddenly and headed rapidly off through the trees and into the distance, his black bag still over his shoulder. It was almost like seeing a ghost, appearing out of nowhere and disappearing without a trace.

I looked down at my mother lying on the ground beside me. She looked peaceful, as if pretending to be asleep, like in one of our imaginary games, ready to wake up at any moment and gaze adoringly into my eyes.

I noticed a piece of paper on the ground nearby, which had fallen from her pocket, and reached down to pick it up, holding it out to her.

'Get up, Mummy!' I said to her.

She didn't respond.

'Get up, Mummy!' I said louder.

Why didn't she move or answer?

'*Get up, Mummy!*' I shouted with all my strength.

In less than a split second, life seemed to have come to a standstill. She was gone. Just like Birdie, she had disappeared. I was very young, and yet, at that moment, on some deep level, I knew that she was never coming back. My heart was completely broken. She was never going to get up and play with me again. I would never look into her loving eyes and see her adoring smile again. I would never hear her soft voice again, telling me how much she loved me.

I reached down and placed the piece of paper delicately upon her forehead so it would be with her wherever she was.

Around me there was absolute silence. The woodland was peaceful. Even though my mother's body lay beside me on the ground. Even though my face was swollen and bruised and my clothes splattered with blood.

I can't say how long I was there. Two minutes? Five? Ten? I knew, however, that there was no reason for me to remain there for even a second longer. I began running out of the woods up onto the grassy slope from which we had come a short while ago. I'm not sure I knew where I was heading but I knew I was going somewhere for a reason. I was flooded with pain, but felt a guiding hand on my shoulder, ushering me gently out of the trees. Suddenly, the bright rays of the morning sun dazzled my eyes as the sounds of families and friends sharing picnics happily together on the grass around me grew louder.

As I emerged from the trees, strangers came running towards me. They must have noticed my battered face and the blood splattered across my clothes. They were kind to me and somehow I knew I could trust them. But it felt like, although I was physically present, inside I was floating somewhere far away.

In my memory, I still hear the sirens wailing in the background. I hear people talking to me, as well as to one another, but the words no longer register. In the distance the first flashing blue lights of police cars appear and when the ambulance arrives I'm rushed inside, sedated by doctors and drift off into a deep sleep.

When I opened my eyes I was lying in a hospital bed; white room, white ceiling, white floor, white walls and green curtains.

The story was already all over the news. Hordes of reporters were surrounding the building and the hospital's staff had been ordered to lock down all floors in order to avoid them breaking in. There were police and security guards posted all across the building.

I was awake, but still in a dreamy state. I lay very still, trying to work out where I was. Soon a nurse appeared, offering me water to drink and biscuits to eat. I didn't ask where my mother was. Inside, part of me was still attempting to understand everything that had happened.

The nurses were warm and friendly, and even though we talked and read some books together the words no longer reach me. How much time passed I don't know. But eventually one of the nurses led me by the hand through a large, echoing hallway to where my father stood at the far end, waiting for me.

He came rushing towards us, lifted me up into his arms and gave me a crushing hug. I gazed intensely and unblinkingly into his eyes. They were red and raw and tears were running down his cheeks.

'There's been a terrible accident,' he began, his voice breaking as he struggled to find the words. 'Mummy has been killed and she's not coming back ...'

CHAPTER 2

OMENS

'The hand that rocks the cradle is the
hand that rules the world.'

William Ross Wallace

One of my earliest memories dates back to a holiday in Crete, the autumn before that July day. My parents and I stayed in a pretty little village near the coast.

In my memory I'm lying on a bed in our apartment, looking up at a naked orange light bulb that sticks out from the wall above my head. I'm fascinated and want to reach out and touch it. A few minutes later I'm screaming at the top of my lungs and my parents come running to see what's happened.

My mother then nurses me lovingly as I feel the after-effect of the burn on my fingertip. I remember it as if it were only yesterday.

During our two-week stay, the three of us went out walking; we visited beautiful deserted beaches, swam in the sea amongst shoals of multi-coloured fish, and I found endless amusement digging in the sand above the shore. At mealtimes we ate delicious food in restaurants run by local families, feeding our leftovers to a stray dog and her eight little puppies that followed us everywhere we went. We had a fantastic time and the days soon flew by.

But one beautiful morning, as we wound our way down to the beach along a sandy road, a dark omen was to cast its shadow across our path.

As my mother wheeled me in my pushchair, the three of us stopped to pick blackberries from the bushes along the trail until my face was covered with sticky juice. All of a sudden, we heard the sound of a sheep bleating desperately in the distance. The sound was deeply disturbing and only grew louder the closer we came.

My parents soon realised that the sheep's head was trapped in a wire fence and my father went running to help. But, no matter how hard he tried, the sheep only managed to ensnare itself deeper and deeper in the wire.

As my father wrestled to set the animal free, he suddenly realised that it had no eyes or ears – the poor creature was an abomination of nature with no visible features at all. Eventually it became more and more distressed, pressing harder and harder until the wire pierced through its skin and blood began to stain its fleece.

Unaware of much of what was going on, I carried on untroubled, stuffing my mouth with as many blackberries as I could from the comfort of my pushchair, but my mother too was becoming distraught. No matter how hard my father tried, he was unable to set the animal free.

'Leave it!' my mother finally exclaimed. She could barely watch, so disturbing did she find the scene.

With regret, my father joined us back on the trail, and as we set off again the sound of bleating began to fade into the distance.

As unsettling as the occurrence had been, it wasn't the only one that was to disturb my father's peace of mind during our stay. Many years later, he would confide in me that visions of men overpowering my mother repeatedly flashed into his head from time to time. They seemed to appear out of the blue and didn't bear any obvious relation to the joy of our idyllic holiday – but my father decided to keep these visions to himself; he knew they would only frighten my mother.

The story goes that their paths had first crossed on a warm summer's day while my father was taking his two younger brothers, Mohan and Chan, out to a water park. Perhaps their meeting was written in the stars because the local pool was closed for maintenance that morning, and my father had decided to drive the boys across town to Richmond baths instead.

While my uncles, who were then nine and eleven, were having the time of their lives throwing themselves down the water slides, my father noticed an attractive young woman working as a lifeguard on the other side. With her feminine aura, and a dazzling smile that radiated beauty and charm, she stopped him in his tracks.

'Can I buy you an ice-cream?' he asked with a big grin, after shooting down a water slide. My mother glanced at him from the raised lifeguard chair above, whistle in hand.

'No,' she replied firmly, turning her head the other way. But despite her attempt to play it cool, my father had glimpsed the trace of a smile.

Soon after, he saw her again and went over. This time she told him that her name was Rachel and that she was 19 years old and studying English literature at university. He introduced himself as André and told her he was 25 and a semi-professional tennis player. They chatted for a while, and despite his brothers giggling and staring, they agreed to meet that evening after work.

After dropping his brothers home, my father drove back across town to meet her. The two of them spent hours walking along the banks of the Thames, getting to know each other and finding out about one another's dreams and passions.

As my father soon found out, my mother had been a national-level swimmer in her youth, riding horses whenever she could, while dreaming about becoming a professional ballet dancer – until she eventually grew too tall. Although she loved being physically active, she also loved books and reading. One of her favourite pastimes, however, was just simply to 'potter around', as she called it, taking it easy, and doing a bit here and there.

As a child she had been very bright, achieving good marks at a girls' grammar school. She'd loved acting and singing, but her heart had been set on dancing and now she wasn't sure what to do next.

For my father, on the other hand, there were no doubts as to what his dreams were made of. He had been in love with tennis since picking up a racket at the age of eight. Growing up in Wimbledon, he dreamed of becoming a champion and idolised a number of tennis greats whom he queued for hours to see in the flesh, including his all-time favourites: Nastase, Borg, McEnroe and Arthur Ashe. He had left home at the age of 17, travelling across the globe with nothing but a rucksack on his back and some tennis rackets under his arm, taking part in tournaments whenever and wherever he could.

In order to fund his travels, he took on a number of different jobs along the way and managed to reach destinations as far away as India and the USA, where he lived in California for a year, as well as spending time in Spain, France, Italy and Portugal.

He had shown real promise, but with no money and no backing his dreams of playing professionally were also on hold, and at the age of 23 he had thought that a little 'speculating' in the real-estate sector would prove to be much more lucrative, so he decided to get into the property market. After buying a run-down flat in Balham he spent the next 10 months plastering, plumbing and painting during the day, while serving drinks behind a bar at night.

He planned on selling as soon as the renovations were completed, but shortly after came the 1987 stock market crash and housing prices collapsed. Unable to sell, he shared the flat with a couple of friends and worked at three jobs to keep up the mortgage payments.

As my parents walked for hours that evening, telling one another about their lives, my father realised that he felt more at ease than he ever had with any woman before. He knew he'd met someone special. My mother felt the same deep connection too; so much so that on the very day they met she telephoned her mother to tell her that she'd just found the man of her life – 'because he drinks a lot of bottled water, like me'!

Soon my parents were inseparable. My father's flatmates moved out, my mother moved in and a few months later they discovered that I was on the way. It was a shock to both of them and they were uncertain about what to do. Each unsure of what the other really wanted, they agreed that an abortion was the sensible thing. With a heavy heart my father rang a friend to borrow the money, but as soon as he mentioned that my mother was pregnant his friend's reaction was to congratulate them enthusiastically. When my father explained to him that they were planning to have an abortion his friend was shocked. He advised them to take some time to think things through, rather than jumping into a decision they might later regret. Listening to those words, something clicked, and in that moment my father realised how much he wanted to keep the baby after all.

All he needed to do was persuade my mother to go along with his plan, but he had a feeling that wasn't going to be hard. He had already seen the flickers of hope in her eyes and felt the burgeoning realisation that perhaps she wanted to keep the baby too. And so, within a few days, they had both decided that this was what they most wanted.

From that very moment my mother threw herself into the role of expectant parent, reading everything she could lay her hands on about pregnancy, birth and bringing up a child.

She would now have to put her studies to one side, but in all truth she had already lost interest in her degree. It had dawned on her some while before that she was just going through the motions and she could no longer find any good reason to continue doing something just for the sake of it. Now, my imminent arrival gave her a new-found sense of purpose and happiness.

Telling her parents that she was pregnant wasn't at all easy for my mother. She knew that they were going to be disappointed and would not approve of her choices. They would have liked her to finish university and marry before having a baby, but she was passionately happy with my father and excited about having a child and she hoped they would understand and respect her wishes.

In the end she decided to write them a letter, hoping that it would give them time to come to terms with the new direction her life was taking.

My father had already been introduced to my mother's family early on and had spent quite a lot of time with them. Her father was director of a shoe company and she had enjoyed a comfortable middle-class upbringing in villages in Devon and Essex. From the very beginning her father had been very welcoming towards my father, enjoying the company of a fellow sportsman. My grandfather had been a great rugby player: as an army officer he had been selected for the armed forces team and had gone on to represent his country.

My father looked on my mother's family as a very tight-knit unit who felt passionately about each other. His own family background had been less than perfect, and he felt happy for my mother. But the news that she had abandoned her studies and was pregnant led to an immediate cooling in her parents' attitude to my father. My grandfather told him that the enormous upset my conventional great-grandmother felt at her granddaughter's fairytale future being thrown out of the window was all because of him.

It probably didn't help that my parents had no intention of marrying. Early on in their relationship they had decided they would spend the rest of their lives together. But for them there would be no showcase wedding. Instead they made an agreement between the two of them – a promise that didn't require documents to be signed or a priest's blessing for their commitment to each other to be lasting and true.

It took my grandparents some time to get over their initial shock and to accept my mother's choices, but eventually they came around and supported her throughout her pregnancy. They too had been through good times as well as bad in the past. Not only had there been plenty of business successes, but also roadblocks and setbacks along the way. 'Just when things are going well, that's when life comes along and slaps you around the back of the head,' my grandfather would comment from time to time.

My father was the son of an English mother and a Zimbabwean father. He had been brought up by his mother until the age of nine, when she moved out, and his father, who up until then had been an irregular presence, moved in. A teacher by profession, he was a critical and distant parent, and the two of them struggled to adapt to their new life. After that my father saw his mother once a month and she went on to have two more sons with her new husband. By the time my parents met, my father was no longer in contact with his father, but his mother was delighted by the prospect of a grandchild and his brothers were excited about becoming uncles.

Both my parents were fit and healthy and my mother's pregnancy went very smoothly, aside from a little morning sickness very early on. Even so, she continued to exercise during the entire nine months, and was swimming up to the very last days before my birth.

Keen as they were for me to arrive, I appeared to be in no hurry. When I was over two weeks late, with still not a twinge of labour, my mother stood in front of a chest of drawers which she had lovingly filled with clothing for me and exclaimed, 'It's all ready for you! All we need is for you to come out and take a look.'

My parents had always referred to me as a 'he' because what my mother most wanted in the world was for me to be a boy. Somehow, ever since she was a little girl, she had always known that one day she would have a son called Alexander Louis. My father, however, wasn't so sure and wanted to consider other names before making a final decision. But in the end my mother was able to convince him, and together they agreed that their son would be given the names of two emperors: Alexander the Great and Louis XIV, the Sun King. It wouldn't be until years later, however, that my father would learn that in Greek Alexander means protector of Andros – the origin of his own name.

After investigating all the options my parents had agreed on a home birth. My mother wasn't keen on hospitals or doctors and felt sure she'd be happier, and the birth would be easier, at home.

I made my way into the world just after 7 am on 11 August 1989, uttering some strange noises that resembled a sort of singing. There were no signs of tears. In fact, I didn't cry for hours. When my mother discovered that I was indeed a boy she was ecstatic. Once the midwife finished her inspection I was put to sleep on a sheepskin in the middle of my parents' bed.

Delirious with exhaustion, my mother awoke suddenly in the middle of the night. 'Something's different!' she exclaimed. 'What is it?' Suddenly, the realisation struck her. 'The baby. Where is he?'

My father began to panic as he looked desperately around the room – but there I was, right where I'd been left, sleeping soundly and without a care in the world, on my sheepskin, lodged safely between my parents in their bed.

From the start I woke frequently during the night, something that showed no signs of changing as I grew older. Nothing made any difference – skipping naps, lots of fresh air, all the standard things were tried. They didn't make any difference: I was simply a high-octane child and didn't need much rest, so my parents had to put up with a lot of sleep deprivation. Especially my mother. But even so, they treasured those early days, the three of us happily nesting in the flat, far from the hectic world outside.

My mother breastfed me and was still feeding me as I approached my third birthday. She believed passionately in the benefits of breastfeeding and a healthy diet and had become vegetarian herself at the age of five, after copying her older brother.

My grandparents used to call her 'Me Too', because she absolutely adored her big brother Mark and would try to copy everything he did. One day, when he was seven, they passed a butcher's shop on the high street and he asked their mother what it was selling. After considering the ramifications of her explanation he vowed never to eat meat again – and my mother insisted: 'Me too!'

She had stuck to that vow ever since, and took great care to ensure that when I started to eat solids my diet was healthy, nutritious and plant-based.

Though my father worked long hours, weekends were a time when the three of us would be together and I always had something fun to look forward to, whether it was a long walk in the countryside, travelling in the Volvo to tennis tournaments in which my father was playing, or helping him to repair his bike on the street outside our flat. One of my favourite toys was a plastic, battery-driven socket set, which I was happy to play with for hours on end – although I always preferred to stick my hand in my father's toolbox whenever I 'helped' him fix his bike.

My father was of course the one with whom I would do the exciting 'boy' things that my mother would cringe at. This often involved being pushed around in something with wheels as I shouted, 'Faster! Faster!' He understood that boys have to do boy things and learn from them just as my mother understood it was better not to make a big deal of it when I hurt myself, but to trust that I would soon pick myself up again and learn from it.

In between, my mother and I visited both sets of grandparents regularly, and on holidays and at Christmas there were more family get-togethers. With all the attention and encouragement I received, it was no surprise that I was always a healthy and precocious baby. By eight months I was already walking, although while my legs were strong my coordination wasn't yet up to the task, so I kept banging into things and everybody had to be on the lookout. I often bumped my head, which led to a lot of crying. Arnica was my wonder remedy, so effective that eventually just the sight of the bottle would act as a placebo, calming me down immediately.

Dressing up was one of my favourite pastimes. I would put on my Fireman Sam costume – yellow trousers, blue tunic with shiny buttons and yellow plastic helmet – and my mother would push me on my tricycle to the park and to the shops. I refused to respond to 'Alex' and insisted on being addressed as 'Fireman Sam', something that would make my face light up with happiness.

By the time I was two my parents decided it would be good for me to grow up with a companion. They both loved dogs, so one weekend the three of us drove out to the countryside to pick up a puppy from an animal shelter. My mother decided to leave it up to me and my father to choose and waited for us in the car while we went down to the end of a long garden, where a large litter of puppies were hurling themselves against the fence of a small enclosure. They were yellow and black Labrador-greyhound cross puppies, and one of them was trampling over the top of all the others, baying for attention.

'We'll have that one!' my father exclaimed. I nodded happily, as the beautiful, shiny black puppy snuffled my hand. My mother named her Molly.

Despite the regular strains that all households and parents suffer from in the modern world – bills to pay, long hours to work and the needs of a demanding child – for my parents and me life was predominantly happy. And yet, for my mother especially, there seemed at times to be a strange sense of foreboding.

On more than one occasion she had asked my father to promise that, if anything ever happened to her, he would find someone else. It was her wish that we both have someone around to look after us. My father found the subject very uncomfortable, but nevertheless promised her that he would. When he turned the tables, however, and asked her what she would do in the event of anything happening to him, she said that while she could see my father clearly as an old, bald man, she could see no image of her future self at all.

There were other occasions when fears weighed upon her. One afternoon, before I was born, my parents went to the cinema together. Only minutes after the film had started, my mother said she needed to go to the toilet, which was just at the end of their row. My father acknowledged her wordlessly and, expecting her to get up and go, was immediately immersed in the film once again. A few minutes later, still seated beside him, my mother repeated that she needed to go to the toilet.

'Why don't you go, then?' my father asked, confused.

'I'm afraid of being attacked from behind. Someone might get me!' she replied.

It was a fear she was to repeat throughout their relationship, although there seemed to be no apparent explanation for it.

'Why did you kill me?' my mother demanded to know on another occasion, when she woke in the middle of the night as if from a dream.

My father stared at her, deeply concerned, attempting to decipher what she meant. Upon awakening fully, my mother explained that in her dream someone whose face she couldn't see was attacking her from behind with a knife.

It was now only a few months later, and my mother's deepest fears had come true. The omens which had once visited us had become a vivid reality, and as my father stood in tears at the end of the hospital hall, holding me in his arms, I was now the only witness to my mother's murder.

CHAPTER 3

A NEW REALITY

'The truth is stranger than fiction.'

Mark Twain

My grandmother had come to the hospital to be with us. She had heard, in a desperate phone call from my father, that my mother was dead. But all she could understand was 'Rachel's been killed', so she had driven all the way across town thinking that my mother must have been involved in some kind of traffic accident. Years later, my father would explain to me that he had taken a break from work earlier that morning to call me and my mother. He called every morning, but for my father that day was especially important. He felt shaken and concerned by my mother's sombre mood. Her words, 'I just want to sleep forever,' still echoed in his mind and he wanted the reassurance of hearing that all was well.

After parking his bike on the street in a break between jobs, he stepped up to a public telephone, placed a coin in the slot and dialled home. The phone rang only a couple of times before it clicked as it was picked up on the other end.

'Hello,' a strange male voice answered. 'Is that André? Are you Rachel's boyfriend?'

My father was thrown. Who could possibly be in our home and not know the answer to that?

'Yes!' he shouted. 'Where is she?'

'André, where are you now?' The stranger replied. 'Don't hang up.'

'Who the hell are you?' my father demanded. 'What are you doing in my house? Where's Rachel?'

'Where are you, André?' the stranger said. 'Are you on your own? Please stay on the phone!'

My father was furious. What was happening? Something had to be terribly wrong.

'Where's Rachel?' he repeated.

'André …' The stranger paused. 'I'm a police officer. I have to tell you there's been a terrible accident.'

My father, inundated by thoughts and images that he fought with all his strength to keep away, could barely respond. 'What's happened?' he whispered.

'Rachel …' The officer's voice began to break. 'Rachel has been attacked while walking on the Common.'

My father's world came crashing down. His heart pounding, he began to shiver uncontrollably.

'Is she dead?' he asked.

'I can't answer that over the phone,' the officer replied.

She was dead: there was no doubt in my father's mind;

otherwise he would have said she was alive. But as much as he knew in that very moment that my mother was gone, part of him could still not believe that this was really happening.

'André, stay where you are,' the officer added. 'Don't move. We'll get a car to you in a few minutes. Just tell me where you are.'

But my father had to know. 'Is she dead?' he insisted.

There was a terrible silence.

'Yes,' came the reluctant answer. 'I'm so sorry, I didn't want to tell you like this.'

'Where's Alex?' There was little hope in my father's voice. He was sure that I must be dead as well.

'He's all right,' the officer replied. 'He's at Wimbledon police station. André, please stay where you are. We'll have somebody with you in just a couple of minutes.'

Somehow he had to let my mother's parents know. But they were away on holiday in Canada and there was no way to reach them. He managed to call his own mother to let her know what had happened, and she set off to meet him at Wimbledon police station.

As my father hung up the phone, he collapsed to the floor and cried uncontrollably. After some time, he managed to stand and calm himself while he waited for the car that the officer had promised would come.

But with no sign of the car, my father decided to make his own way to the nearest police station, a few minutes away. He didn't want me to be without him for any longer than necessary.

As soon as he parked his bike and entered the building he explained to the desk sergeant who he was and why he was there – but to his astonishment he was immediately met with hostility and made to wait. The minutes passed. His mind was consumed with thoughts; all he wanted was to get to me. After a time he was taken to the back of the building behind closed doors, where a policewoman stared him down. 'I've been told what you said when you came into the station. A police officer would never have told you that on the phone.'

A misguided perception had led the officers in charge to assume, from my father's distressed state and physical appearance, with his shaven head and leather overalls, that he could only be some kind of madman.

'We've been trying to get through to Wimbledon to find out what's going on,' the officer continued, 'but this just doesn't sound right. This isn't the way that we do things.'

After a long, uncomfortable detainment, the officer in charge finally gave permission for him to be released.

With little choice, he clambered back on his bike, determined to get to Wimbledon police station as soon as possible.

His mind was reeling. He stopped at some traffic lights and found himself staring at his reflection in the darkened back window of a London taxi. For the whole ride his mind had been split between two planes, on one level struggling to come to terms with reality while on another he focused completely on the mechanics of what he was doing in greater detail than ever before.

Watch out for the bus on the roundabout. That car looks like it will cut you up if it gets half a chance, don't give him a gap, keep in front of him or get out of his way completely. Second gear, third gear, fourth gear. That's enough. Take it easy. Knock off the speed, your reactions are slow, you can't afford to drive that fast.

Now, as he sat watching his reflection, another part of his mind was considering what practical method he would use to end both our lives. Without my mother, he felt there was nothing left for either of us to live for. He missed her so much already that he could hardly breathe, and he was convinced that there was no way I would want to carry on without her. My mother and I adored each other so much that we seemed joined together, inseparably, as one unit.

On the way he stopped at a small greengrocer, to buy some grapes. He wanted to bring something nice for me and it gave him more reason than ever to drive carefully, so that he wouldn't squash or bruise them.

The amount of effort and willpower my father exerted to keep himself together during the journey was enormous, but somehow he made it to the other end in one piece.

As soon as he entered the police station in Wimbledon, however, he was told that I wasn't there after all, and again he was made to wait. He was boiling inside with rage, but before he could erupt, two detectives in civilian clothes emerged and, leading him into a quiet back room, informed him of the circumstances of my mother's death with great sensitivity.

My father cried uncontrollably as he was told that my mother had been stabbed over and over again. Images of her being attacked with a knife flashed repeatedly through his mind, and all he could do was wish with all his heart that it had been him instead. 'How could my baby have endured such suffering?' he wondered in anguish.

The detectives drove him to the hospital and, as he sat in the back of the unmarked car, they did their best to prepare him for the scene that was to come. 'I have to warn you that there is already a lot of press interest,' one of them explained. My father could only wonder what that meant. But as soon as they drew into the hospital's car park he realised that the entire building was surrounded by reporters and photographers, and the two detectives and my father were forced to enter incognito through a back door and use the service lift.

When the elevator doors opened, the matron in charge appeared and explained to my father that I was in one of the smaller wards in the care of a nurse and a policewoman. She said that I had been given a sedative and would be asleep for quite some time. My father knew that my mother would have wanted me to have my own special things to help me through such an overwhelming moment, so one of the detectives offered to drive him back to our flat to collect them before I awoke.

Before leaving, my father carried out the heart-wrenching task of calling my uncle Mark, the brother my mother had adored so much, to break the news. Struggling to take in the news himself, my uncle promised to try to get hold of my grandparents before making his way to the hospital.

My father arrived at our flat only to find the door knocked down by the police. Without stopping to think, he grabbed a bag and began to fill it with clean clothes, my blankets, my small knife and fork, my favourite plate, my Fireman Sam videos, my treasured story books and toys – and most important of all, my sheepskin. It had been with me since my birth and always came with us whenever we slept away from home.

He started to make a mental shopping list: dried apricots and cashew nuts for snacks, the little packets of juice with the straw that I liked. What else did my mother get for me? Pasta for lunch, veggie burgers, baked potatoes, peanut butter on toast.

Would this give me the message that everything was still there for me – that only one part of my life, even if it was the most important part, had been ripped away?

When he returned to the hospital, his mother was already there with Molly and my uncles Mohan and Chan. They could barely take in what had happened. Both of them had been there the day my parents met four years before, and adored my mother.

A child psychologist was to arrive to offer some advice before my father was allowed to see me. In the meantime the matron informed him that I had eaten some biscuits and looked at some books. She told him that I had been very calm and well behaved. My father, however, couldn't imagine any circumstances in which I would have remained calm if forced away from my mother.

The wait for the psychologist was excruciating, but when he finally arrived he urged my father to make sure that I was left in no doubt whatsoever that my mother was dead. Children were capable of recovering from the most terrible of circumstances, he said, but what gives them a base to do so is not to be overloaded with affection and toys but the honest truth and a solid routine.

Minutes later, I gazed intensely into my father's eyes. The signs of recent violence were unmistakable; there were cuts and bruises on my face.

I looked at him as if to say, 'I know she's dead. I know she's not coming back.' But, following the psychologist's advice, my father persisted. 'There has been a terrible accident,' he began, his voice breaking as he struggled to find the words. 'Mummy has been killed and she is not coming back …'

I hadn't said a word.

'But we're going on together,' he continued. 'Daddy's here for you now … and I've got your blankets here, and your sheepskin's here, and Grandma June's here and Mohan and Chan are here, and your Uncle Mark's here and Grandma and Grandpa will be back soon, and we're going to stay at Grandma June's house with Molly, and we'll get your toys …'

As my grandmother drove us from the hospital across town to her home in North London, I sat in the back of her car gazing silently through the window, eating the grapes my father had brought for me, while Molly dozed quietly with her head on my lap.

Sitting beside me, his mind was consumed with thoughts: 'How long will a recovery from this kind of trauma take? And what are the chances of him living any kind of normal life again?' he wondered.

They were questions that would plague him continuously throughout the weeks and months to come.

Because my grandmother had remarried years before, the press wouldn't be able to track us down by our family surname, at least for now. The story was already all over the news, and reporters were voraciously hunting for leads across London, pursuing anybody with the slightest connection to our family. There were reporters watching our flat, and the parents of the children I went to nursery with had been chased down the street on their way out of school. Sooner or later they would find out where we were – but for now we were safe.

'Daddy!' I cried as I awoke suddenly, in the middle of the night. It was the first night of my life without my mother.

In the past, whenever I awoke it was always my mother that I called for. But seamlessly, I had now changed from one to the other. Immediately, my father climbed out of his bed and came over to mine in the bedroom we now shared in my grandmother's house. But by the time he arrived I was deeply asleep once more. Had I even been truly awake?

In the early hours of the morning the nightmares began, their unwelcome arrival marking the beginning of a repetitive pattern in our daily life together over the years to come. On the other side of the room my father awoke suddenly once again. The sounds emerging from me were so disturbing that they scraped his nerves raw. This wasn't normal crying but a completely alien sound, primal and terrifying in its distress. My movements were jerky and spasmodic and I seemed broken and deranged.

In almost three years of life I had slept peacefully every night, often chortling and laughing out loud in a way that filled my parents with joy and wonder – they had prided themselves on how happy I so obviously was. But now I sounded like a dying animal. I was trapped inside a horrifying nightmare and my father couldn't snap me out of it. My eyes were screwed tightly shut and I was still deep in a sleep state. 'Look what you have taken from me!' he screamed silently in his head. 'Look what you have left me with: this broken child.'

Eventually, he managed to lift me up and cradle me in his arms. As he held me close, he began what was soon to become a familiar litany of reassurance. My whole body continued to spasm intensely, but after some time I began to calm down.

When I finally opened my eyes I was subdued, and my father put me back on my bed to recover. As I lay there silently, gazing at the ceiling, he began to stroke my hair. He told me he loved me, that Grandma June loved me, that my other grandma and my grandpa loved me. And that Molly loved me.

'Everyone dies some time,' he began, 'but nearly everyone gets old and tired before they die. Hardly anyone dies when they're young like Mummy. This was just a terrible, terrible accident. Just look how old Grandma and Grandpa are, and they're not dead yet!'

He paused. At that moment all he needed was the slightest hint of permission from me to end both our lives.

'One day Molly will be too old to run around. She'll be tired, and will just want to sleep. And one day she just won't wake up any more.'

'I want to wake up!' I said quietly.

Although I still gazed at the ceiling, my words were spoken with absolute clarity and conviction.

Speechless, my father stared at the side of my head, stunned. This wasn't at all the response he had expected. Without the slightest hesitation, I was telling him that even after everything that had happened I wanted to go on. My words took my father's breath away and at that moment he knew there was no other option. Somehow we had to continue together.

'Then you will,' he said softly. 'You won't die until you are very, very old.'

Outside, dawn was breaking, and the first day of a new life without my mother was about to begin.

CHAPTER 4

THE ROSE

'He who has a "why" to live, can bear
with almost any "how".'

Friedrich Nietzsche

'Where are we going?' I asked my father as we sat together in the back seat of my grandmother's car. It was mid-morning and the rush-hour traffic had just died away. Molly was lying close beside me and Justine, one of my mother's closest girlfriends, sat beside my grandmother as she drove.

'For a walk,' he replied.

Since collecting me from the hospital the previous afternoon, I hadn't let him out of my sight for even a second. Now, in an attempt to re-establish a sense of normality and some kind of routine that we could build upon amidst the chaos unfolding around us, we were heading to Hampstead Heath.

The evening before, three detectives had arrived to question him and to ask him to hand over address books, details of my parents' bank accounts, family photographs, and both his and my mother's diaries.

As I slept upstairs, my first nightmares lurking beneath the surface, the police subjected him to a gruelling list of questions: Who did my parents know? Who did my mother see? When had my father left the house? Did they owe anybody money? Did they have any enemies? Could my father prove his whereabouts? Did my mother have any life insurance? Was my mother wearing any jewellery? Did my father know what my mother's movements were that morning? What did my mother normally do? What had she done the day before? When was the last time we had all gone to the Common together? Had my father seen anything that made him suspicious? What were our movements the night before? When had they last made love? What contraceptives did they use?

Although the press were yet to discover our whereabouts, the story had appeared in every major newspaper that morning and was being broadcast at regular intervals by every television station in the country. Meanwhile members of my mother's family were still to be informed.

After numerous attempts my uncle Mark was still unable to reach his parents, who remained isolated on an extended boat trip somewhere in Canada.

He had spent the night on the sofa downstairs, trying to get what rest he could and had left before sunrise, anxious to reach his parents' house in Bedfordshire as soon as possible. My grandmother's elderly mother was staying there on her own, feeding the cats while my grandparents were away on holiday.

The police had warned him not to leave her alone for long in case reporters tried to break in to steal whatever family photographs they could find. They had already surrounded the house and were constantly knocking at the door and ringing the phone. The officers had also explained that it was common practice in these cases for the press to stroll into the local pharmacy, presenting themselves as members of the family, in order to steal whatever negatives they might have recently left to be developed.

Despite everything that had happened the previous day, and in spite of the nightmares that had tormented me that night, I had slept deeply and woken up eager to get on with my day.

Even at just under three, I was already something of a perfectionist and everything had to be just right for me. But my mother, who knew how to prepare everything for me in just the way I liked, was no longer beside me to see to my needs, and at breakfast my father struggled to find his footing until I instructed him which cup to use for my juice, the amount of peanut butter I wanted spread on my toast, and how I wanted both blankets wrapped around me as I wandered through the house.

When we arrived at the Heath, I was eager to have a good time. It was a place I knew well; a large stretch of open ground, similar to Wimbledon Common. As we climbed out of the car, clouds rolled across the sky. Despite the bright morning sun, a storm was brewing.

My father didn't want me to have too much time to think, or to associate what had happened to my mother with the surroundings in which it had occurred, otherwise I might never be able to go to a park or open space again.

But despite his concerns, I seemed perfectly relaxed. Without a backward glance, I went running to explore under the branches of trees, in surroundings uncannily similar to those in which I had witnessed my mother's murder only twenty-four hours before.

With my grandmother and Justine, we played all the games that were part of my world. Pretending to be trains, like those in the Thomas the Tank Engine stories I loved so much, we ran around together, racing back and forth. Afterwards I threw sticks for Molly to chase and spelled out the letters I was able to recognise among those inscribed on the surrounding benches.

My father was torn; relieved that I seemed happy, but puzzled that I did not appear more traumatised. 'Why doesn't he break down and cry?' he wondered, unable to hold back his own tears while watching me entertaining myself as if nothing had happened.

On the way back to my grandmother's house, we stopped at a shopping centre to pick up a few books and tapes, some paper and crayons for me to draw with and some kits to build. The kind of things that my father knew my mother would have wanted me to have.

When we got back to the house, we all sat in the living room together, and I climbed on my father's lap to watch a video. The cover blurb had seemed reassuring, and had been along the lines of 'a charming and gentle story for small children that parents can allow them to watch and enjoy with peace of mind'. But within minutes I was in tears. The story involved a nation of rhinoceroses waging war on a nation of elephants. The rhinos stormed across the elephants' land, tearing down houses and kidnapping the mothers and baby elephants that huddled fearfully inside. Still holding me, my father leapt up to turn off the TV. From the other side of the room Justine stared at him, shocked. It was exactly the kind of trigger they had intended to avoid.

My distress soon passed, though, and within a matter of minutes I was playing happily with a vacuum cleaner at the bottom of the staircase. At the top of the stairs, my father sat quietly with Justine and one of his closest male friends who had just arrived. For the first time all day he seemed to be finding some kind of respite after everything that had happened.

'You've got a pip in your heart!' I announced suddenly at the top of my voice, as I climbed the stairs with the vacuum in my hand.

'Have I?' my father replied, stunned. Before my mother died, a seed had embedded itself in one of Molly's ears, causing her great discomfort. At the time, I had wanted to know all about it.

'You've got a pip in your heart and I'm going to get it out!' I exclaimed as I forced the end of the vacuum to his chest.

Our two friends were speechless.

'I've got to get it out because it hurts!' I declared. I wouldn't let him move one bit, and even made him lift up his shirt so that I could press the hose directly to his heart. For the next twenty minutes I hummed like a vacuum cleaner while studying him intently. If he made the slightest attempt to get up, I would insist he sit down again. Finally, when I was at last satisfied with the operation, with a big smile on my face, I happily informed my father that the pip was out.

* * *

Years later, my father explained to me that the scene had left our friends speechless.

'It was incredible,' they said to my father later that evening. 'How could a small child understand what a heart is and the significance it has for people? And how incredibly generous of him to want to take the pain of another person away … He could have just got on with playing with his toys or done anything else to distract himself instead …'

Guided by instinct, or some deeper understanding, I had done more for my father than I could possibly know.

The next morning I woke up early and made my way into my father's bed. 'Mine, mine, mine!' I murmured as I patted him gently on the chest, without disturbing his sleep.

When he finally awoke, we made our way quietly to breakfast and I followed him down the stairs, carrying my blankets with me. Despite the early hour it was already light, but everyone else was still asleep. My uncles were sharing a room on the top floor, and my grandmother and her husband Brijinder slept in their bedroom on the ground floor. At the other side of the house, in the extension, Molly lay sleeping with their two white West Highland Terriers.

After many visits, I was more than familiar with the big, old, rambling Victorian house. To me it seemed like a giant castle with endless corners to explore.

'Where's Celeste?' I asked my father as we made our way into the kitchen. Although I had my own understanding of where my mother was, I wanted to know more, I wanted my father's explanation. But he didn't reply.

'Where's Celeste?' I asked again, gently.

Lost for words, my father didn't even dare turn around. The afterlife is one of the greatest mysteries and for my father it was impossible to offer me an explanation. After breakfast, however, an idea occurred to him, and from the extension beside the dogs he brought out a box of animals to play with on the floor.

'This is Babar,' he said, pointing to the baby elephant. 'Who's that?'

'Me!' I grinned.

'And this is Celeste,' he said, pointing to the mother elephant. 'Who's that?'

'Mummy!' I grinned again with excitement. I was enjoying the game.

My father paused for a moment before going on. Tentatively, he began, 'I know that when Celeste was killed there was somebody else, somebody I don't know ...'

My father had once read an article about a man who used some toys to tell his grandson a story in which a nasty character played the role of a villain whose life came to a sticky end. After the story was finished, all the toys had been put back in their place. But the little boy hadn't forgotten, and the toy that had represented the baddie became an object of fear. Over time the little boy became more and more disturbed by the presence of the threatening figure, whose eyes seemed to follow him all around the house, until finally his grandfather had no choice but to destroy it in order for his grandson to regain his sense of security.

Picking up a piece of paper, my father began to draw a gingerbread man with a knife in his hand.

'This is the man that killed Mummy,' he said, placing it on

the floor beside the two elephants. 'He is a bad, bad man and I hate him. This is what I want to do with him!'

My eyes widened as he grabbed the piece of paper and scrunched it up violently in his hands. I stared towards him, totally enthralled by his performance.

'And this is what I want to do with it!' he exclaimed. 'Do you want to see?'

Without hesitation, I jumped to my feet and followed him closely out of the room and into the kitchen.

'This is what I'm going to do with him!' he exclaimed fiercely, as he squeezed the ball of paper into his hand and slammed it straight into the bin.

Squealing with delight, I began to bounce around the room, laughing loudly.

'Shall we do it again?' he asked.

'Yes!' I replied at once as we rushed back into the extension to do it all over again. Once more I followed him into the kitchen and once more I squealed with joy as he threw the scrunched-up drawing into the bin.

The next time, when he had sketched out the figure again, he asked me, 'What do *you* want to do with the man who killed Mummy?'

Without uttering a word I immediately leapt to my feet, pounded the drawing into a little ball, ran into the kitchen as fast as I could and slammed it into the bin with all my strength. At that moment my father was overcome with a sense of pride. It was the first time I'd left his sight since he'd collected me at the hospital 36 hours earlier.

For the rest of the morning my father drew the same figure over and over again; and over and over again I scrunched it up tightly in my hands and went running into the kitchen on my own to throw it into the bin with all my strength.

The next day, the police arrived to drive us to the hospital. As we sat in the back of an unmarked car, my father explained to me that we were going to see my mother's body. 'She has gone now, sweetheart,' he explained. 'What's left behind is just the shell, it's just like old clothing. It's not her any longer.'

But I showed no enthusiasm at the idea of seeing her body, and hadn't even looked at my father as he talked. For the whole drive I gazed silently out through the open window, my mind somewhere else. When we finally arrived I continued to show the same lack of curiosity. Sitting on my father's lap in the waiting room, however, my interest was soon captured by a tank full of ornamental fish that stood at the far end. Tired of waiting, I climbed down to take a look.

Fascinated by the elegance of the fish and by the way the light flashed when they turned suddenly, I stood glued to the side of the tank while behind me my father waited quietly with my grandmother and a family friend. Eventually a nurse arrived to guide us through to the room where my mother's body lay. I followed my father closely behind, but hung back by the curtain as he walked over to the body.

'My poor baby,' he whispered. 'What you must have been through ...' As he stroked her hair, tears began to fall from his eyes.

'Don't you want to say goodbye to Mummy's body?' he asked as he stretched his arms out towards me. But I didn't want to. After all, my mother was no longer there.

Hesitantly I stood, studying him for a few seconds, before reluctantly walking forward and allowing him to lift me up. I glanced sideways for a moment and then looked away again. Resting on a table, the body lay on its back, wrapped from neck to toe in a robe that left only vague contours visible. There was no sign of any wounds, and her face looked like wax.

'Can we go now?' I asked.

'In a minute,' he replied. 'I want to say goodbye.'

Holding me in his arms, he bent over and kissed her forehead. But when he stood up again he showed no sign of wanting to leave. At that moment my grandmother walked in and took his hand. His eyes were filled with tears.

'Do you want to look at the aquarium again?' my grandmother asked me softly.

I walked towards the door beside her, but turned around again as we reached the curtain. 'When are we going?' I asked my father impatiently. In my mind there was no reason to be there for even a minute longer.

After one last kiss he moved towards us. Lifting me into his arms, he turned back again to take a final look. I glanced back, too, before he carried me out of the door and we headed towards the exit.

The next few days passed in a blur. I remember them only in snatches – playing on the floor with my toys while my father answered phone call after phone call. Although I was perfectly comfortable with everyone in the house, I still didn't let him out of my sight for even a moment. Molly and the little Westies wandered around the house all the while, but I hardly paid them any attention.

One evening, after reading my bedtime story, my father began to stroke my hair and sing to me as I lay in bed. It was an everyday ritual for him to sing gentle soul ballads and jazz standards until I drifted off to sleep. But that evening I lay as if in a trance, silently staring into space. I felt sad, and despite my calmness my father was becoming concerned.

'You're thinking about Mummy, aren't you?' he asked.

Without looking towards him, I moved my chin up and down ever so slightly.

'Your mummy loved you more than anything in the whole world, you know. She didn't want to leave you. She would never have left you … She would have done anything not to leave you. But that man killed her. It wasn't her fault. She was taken away from you.'

There was a loud bang. The bedroom door slammed shut. A thunderstorm had been brewing for days and outside the window the sky was heavy with clouds, but until now there had been no wind.

'She'll always be with you,' my father continued. 'No matter what, for all your life. All the time you're growing up and even when you become a daddy too. She will always find a way to get through to you.' He paused, to recapture his thoughts. So far I had made no acknowledgement, but my father knew I was listening intently.

'Some people say that we come back as animals or even as other people. Mummy always used to say that she was a dolphin before she was born, swimming in the sea. Maybe she'll be a dolphin again. She'd like that. Maybe she'll be a beautiful flower. Whatever it is, she will be part of the good things around you. When the wind blows through your hair, it will feel like her stroking your head. And maybe, when the sun shines and you feel nice and warm, that will be Mummy trying to make you feel nice. When we go to the beach and you swim in the sea, you'll feel her too. When the waves push all around you, she'll be there, looking after you, in the ocean with the fishes.'

I felt the trace of a smile on my lips. Just enough for my father to see that his words were striking a chord.

'And when it rains, part of the rain will be Mummy too. When the rain falls down all clean and new, we will think of her. And when it splashes on the ground, the sound will be like she's singing to you ...'

Suddenly the bedroom window slammed shut; there was a loud clap of thunder and the rain came pouring down. I found my father's words comforting, but the signs being sent to me were even more deeply reassuring. In the background the thunder continued to rumble, and in a matter of seconds I drifted off into a deep, peaceful sleep.

The next morning I made my way down the stairs and found a beautiful, dark red rose on the living room table.

'This is for Mummy,' my father told me as he noticed my fascination. 'I picked it for her from the garden.'

I beamed.

'Do you want to smell it?' he asked, as he handed it to me.

'Nice!' I exclaimed.

My father nudged the rose, still in my hand, against my cheek and I could feel how soft the petals were against my skin. It had a smooth, velvety texture. I like it so much that I didn't want to give it back.

'But it's for Mummy,' he explained.

'It *is* Mummy!' It was just like the story he had told me the night before. 'It's for me!'

My father had picked the rose to place it on the Common, on the spot where my mother had left her body.

'Do you want one for yourself?' he asked.

'Yes!'

In the garden, we found a pretty little rose that was just opening and plucked it gently off the bush together. Holding it carefully in my hand I followed my father back inside. At the kitchen sink, he picked me up so I could fill a jar with water, and after putting the rose in the jar we placed it on the living room table.

For the rest of the day I took great pleasure in explaining to every new arrival that this was 'my mummy'. I proudly insisted that they smell it and feel its cool, velvety petals.

My interest in the rose was to remain just as intense during the following days, and, seeing how enamoured I was becoming, my father started to worry that it would soon fade and that this would make me sad. Taking me aside, he gently began to explain: 'The rose's petals will fade and fall into the earth. They will feed next year's flowers in turn, and in due time those new flowers will blossom and their own petals will also drop into the earth, repeating the same cycle of life over and over again, throughout time.'

I listened intently as my father spoke. His words left a deep impression upon me.

'I'm going to where Mummy was killed so that I can leave this flower for her,' my father told me the next morning as we sat in the back of an unmarked police car. We were parked on a quiet residential street behind Wimbledon police station and I had been looking after the rose for most of the journey. He wanted to visit the place where my mother had spent the last moments of her life, and had been explaining his plans to me all morning. On the way we had stopped to collect Justine and another of my mother's childhood girlfriends, who I was also very fond of.

'I want to come!' I said, as lightly as if they were just heading across the street to buy an ice cream.

The adults in the car went silent and the atmosphere was suddenly charged.

My father had assumed that the place where my mother was killed would be the last place on earth I would want to go. He had expected me to become deeply upset when it was time for him to leave the car and attempt to stop him. He had hoped that with a little coaxing I might be happy to wait for him in the car, with my mother's friends.

'But sweetheart,' he continued, 'I'm going to where Mummy was killed because I wasn't there. You were there, and Molly was there, but I wasn't there. I'm only going to be a few minutes. I'm going to leave this flower for Mummy and then I'll be back and then we can go home.'

'I want to come!' I repeated, this time even more insistently.

My father explained the same thing to me again, and again I give him the same answer.

He was completely thrown: I wasn't saying, 'I don't want you to leave me on my own,' or even 'I don't want you to go.' I was saying that I wanted to come.

'What do you think?' my father asked the detective sitting behind the steering wheel, who was the father of two small children himself.

'He seems to know what you're going to do,' he said quietly. 'He looks as if he really wants to come.'

'That's what I think,' my father replied. 'And if he understands and wants to come then he has to come.'

The detective nodded in agreement.

Until this moment my father had thought that taking a child back to the scene of a crime would be completely crazy, but somehow it now seemed like a good idea. I was thrilled, and sat in the back seat beaming. All the adults present, however, were stunned by my behaviour.

'I'll go and organise a few things,' said the detective, climbing out of the car. 'I'll be back in a minute.'

A few moments later he returned. 'I've managed to arrange it,' he said.

'Thanks,' my father replied.

'But apparently there's going to be some press.'

My father turned the phrase over in his mind. He didn't know exactly what 'some press' might signify. Although they were still camped outside our flat and the story had continued to dominate the front pages and TV screens across the country, so far they hadn't been able to track us down.

We pulled away, and another unmarked police car followed closely behind.

When we reached the Common, uniformed officers on duty appeared to let us into the car park. A mobile incident room had been placed there on the morning of the attack, and it was now closed to the public.

A pathology report had confirmed that my mother had been stabbed a total of 49 times and sexually assaulted. Tapings had been taken from her body to establish if the assailant had left any fibres during the attack – but all that had been found was a footprint and some flecks of red paint in my hair. The investigation had been named 'Operation Edzell' and was quickly becoming one of the largest ever mounted. But a solid lead as to the identity of the man responsible for my mother's death remained elusive. The Common was now under heavy surveillance and everyone's movements were being recorded. There was always a chance that the killer would return.

During the journey the detective had explained that a nearby spot had been marked by the police to allow well-wishers to leave flowers. It was now heaped with beautiful offerings from people who had been so moved by what had happened that they had gone out of their way to show support. Without my knowing it, people from all across the country were praying for my recovery.

The spot where the attack took place was still some distance away, and as we stepped out of the car into the rain my mother's girlfriends tried to block off the first barrage of photographers who had jumped the fence. They had been camped nearby since the morning of the attack and the moment they realised who we were there was a frenzied stampede. They threw themselves at us, thrusting their huge lenses into our faces, while my mother's girlfriends and a few policemen did their best to keep them from trampling us.

All I could hear were the sounds of scuffling feet and the rattling of shutters.

My father lifted me into his arms and covered my face with a baseball cap as we hurried on, pushing against the photographers and reporters who now harried us from both sides. 'We're going to go to the place where Mummy was killed,' he whispered into my ear reassuringly, 'and then we're going to leave the flower for Mummy, and then we'll be going home. We're not going to be very long, and then this afternoon we can go and do something nice and play with your toys.'

He walked on as fast as he could. Soon we passed the spot where Birdie was buried, and the open area where I had run out of the trees. All the while my father continued to whisper reassurances to me. 'Daddy's with you and the police are here to look after you. The bad man has gone. He'd be very frightened if he saw all of us here ...' But despite the chaos unfolding around us, I remained calm. The sights and scenes were all familiar; nearby the stream burbled gently, and when I looked through the canopy above I could see the hollows between the trees. Some distance behind, the police had managed to stop the photographers and reporters from continuing any further along the path behind us. For a few brief seconds we were alone.

'Is this the place?' my father asked.

'Yes,' I nodded confidently. He put me down and held my hand as we laid the rose on the ground together. We stood silently and, dry-eyed, I watched my father crying.

Moments later he lifted me into his arms again. 'It's all right,' he said reassuringly. He knew what was coming and attempted to prepare me as best he could. 'We're going back now. There's something nice to eat in the car and then we'll soon be home for lunch ...'

We had barely emerged from the trees when the hordes of press surrounded us again. I held tightly on to my father as he covered my face with his baseball cap once again. Their voices rang in my ears and, with my field of vision limited, I felt them jostling us on each side, my father struggling to stay on his feet as we wrestled our way back to the car.

On the edges of the car park, one of my mother's girlfriends had just intervened in a verbal altercation between a policeman and a photographer before it came to blows. The officer was upset to the point of tears.

'Why don't you bastards just leave them alone?' he pleaded. But the lenses were shoved towards us unrelentingly. Finally, we clambered back into the unmarked police car, slammed the door shut, and drove off into the distance.

Later that afternoon, my maternal grandparents Andrew and Monica came to meet us at a central London hotel where a press conference was to take place. Almost a week had passed since my mother's death but, given the amount of time it had taken my uncle to reach them and the hours of travelling involved, they had only just landed at the airport earlier that morning.

They had returned to their family's house in Canada, after a boat trip of several days, to find a note pinned to their door by the local sheriff requesting that they contact his office as soon as possible. My grandparents knew immediately that someone in the family had died. They prepared themselves as best they could for the shock and concluded that it must be my great-grandmother, who was already in her eighties, that had passed away. Only when my uncle finally managed to speak to them did they hear the devastating news that it was in fact their daughter.

I was asleep when they arrived at the hotel, but soon I began to stir and woke upset and crying. I was very fond of my grandmother Monica but not even her presence was enough to brighten my mood. Eventually I calmed down with their promise of something nice to eat and drink.

The police had already briefed them on the state of the investigation and my father had also explained to them all that he had learned, and the extent to which the media was intruding into every aspect of our lives.

My grandparents concluded that the best thing to do would be to give the press an opportunity to interview them directly and allow for some photographs to be taken. They assumed, reasonably, that we would then be left alone.

Before the press conference began, we made our way back to my grandmother June's house, my father checking constantly in the rear-view mirror to make sure we weren't being followed. Later that afternoon, before a room packed with reporters, my grandfather paid tribute to my mother's memory. He made a plea for me to be left alone to recover from my ordeal and asked for our privacy as a family to be respected.

That evening my grandfather's speech was broadcast on all main TV channels and radio stations across the country. But the very next morning, against all commonly accepted ideas of moral decency or legality, a major newspaper published a full-face colour picture of me, taken during our visit to the Common.

My safety was now in even greater jeopardy – a physical reminder existed identifying me as the only witness to my mother's murder. The killer remained on the loose, ready to strike again at any moment.

CHAPTER 5

THE CHILD
PSYCHOLOGIST

'An error does not become truth by reason of
multiplied propagation, nor does truth become
error because nobody sees it.'

Mahatma Gandhi

Within a few days of my mother's death, the extension of
the house – where I spent most of my time playing –
had been filled with enough video and sound equipment to
make a feature-length film. There were cameras, microphones
and cables stretching all around the outskirts of the room,
which the police had attempted to conceal behind the furniture
and fittings.

They didn't want to miss a word I might say. Despite the fact
that there were more than 500 people on the Common on
the morning of the attack, no substantial evidence had been
found, nor information uncovered, about the assailant or his

whereabouts. Almost everyone present that morning had been tracked down and interviewed to establish their movements and what, or who, they might have seen. But so far there were no leads and the police were becoming desperate.

Two detectives had now been assigned the task of extracting information from me and although I had taken a liking to them, neither of them were specialists in this field and had simply been appointed by their superiors because they were parents of young children themselves. So far I had not been asked a single question about what took place that morning. The detectives' strategy seemed to be that I would say something important which they would capture on video. By now their faces were becoming familiar. They would drop by the house regularly and I'd watch them out of the corner of my eye while I played and they talked to my father at the other end of the room. They reassured him constantly that although no substantial evidence had been found, they both held the officers in charge of the day-to-day running of the investigation in very high regard, referring to them as people who were 'very thorough' and 'examined every possibility'.

I wasn't upset in the slightest by their presence. As far as I was concerned they spoke when they were spoken to, passed me something if I needed it, and they were a good audience if I decided to sing or perform. Anyone who came into the house had to be extremely careful of what they said in my presence, and my father went out of his way to explain this. Nonetheless, I would sometimes pick up what someone was saying on the other side of the room while appearing to be totally engrossed in something else entirely. If my father happened to mention a dinosaur exhibition, for instance, I was sure to take it in, and wouldn't fail to bring up the subject later. 'When are we going to see the dinosaurs?' I would ask. I never missed a trick, so my father often had to reply to the detectives' questions in vague and unspecific ways.

It wasn't long before I had both detectives down on the floor on all fours joining in with whatever I was doing. When I asked people, 'Do you want to play with me?' the question was purely rhetorical. There was no room for refusal. Both my parents had noticed very early on that I liked adults best. I was never that enthusiastic about other children's company; unable to capture my interest fully, they were only fun for a while. Adults, however, seemed more fun and always able to come up with something new.

I was accustomed to directing my parents in plays, and if Fireman Sam was the game of the day then everyone had to maintain character. They weren't allowed to let their voices drop for an instant. My mother often told my father that she got some funny looks pushing a toddler along in the street in a fireman uniform while talking in a barmy Welsh accent.

Although I possessed a great deal of charm, I was completely tyrannical in my approach, and temper tantrums would ensue if I was not obeyed. It wasn't a surprise for my father, then, to see these two stocky detectives, several times my size, on their knees. Whatever my future occupation might be, my father concluded that I could only be the boss. In his eyes, my man-management ability was already approaching an art form.

One morning the detectives came into the house, accompanied by two women from a child protection team. The younger woman was a police officer in her twenties, and the older was a social worker in her late forties. The detectives had told my father that the social worker had been successful in prompting young children to describe their experiences in cases of sexual abuse.

By the time the visitors arrived, I was already in the extension playing on the floor with my toys. But as soon as my father invited them into the room, I turned my back on them and headed straight into my tent. I had built myself this fortress by turning some chairs upside down and hanging a sheet over the top. I would disappear underneath, giggling, and then reappear, convinced that no one had known where I'd been. I even took my snacks and drinks inside as I sat on my own, playing with toys for hours on end. Only my father and my grandmothers were allowed to enter; if anyone else tried to crawl in, even my uncles, I would push them away with all my strength.

Various members of the family came and went that morning, and I continued to play as far away from the visitors as possible. Outside my tent, the detectives hung about the edges of the room, while from the sofa the younger policewoman tried to make conversation with my father, who was sitting on the floor. She hovered and peered down at me before eventually asking, 'What are you doing there, Alex?'

But I wasn't interested, and didn't even bother to reply. Ignoring people was a tactic I often employed when I didn't appreciate their company. Eventually, one of the detectives who had been trying to catch my father's attention signalled him towards the kitchen. I tracked them from the corner of my eye.

'I don't think we're getting anywhere with these two,' the detective commented.

My father nodded in agreement. 'They've got to go,' he replied. 'They're hopeless.'

I was glad to see them leave that morning – but it was only to be the first of a series of unwelcome visits with so-called experts.

Soon afterwards, the two detectives drove my father and me to Hampstead Heath for our morning walk. Close to my grandmother's house, our visits were now becoming regular. It was a warm, relaxing summer's day when we arrived and we had the Heath virtually all to ourselves. After finding a comfortable spot, the four of us settled down on the grass together and I made myself comfortable on my father's lap. The detectives had brought along some dolls which had been used in cases of child abuse. They were like puppets: males and females of different ages and skin colours; child dolls, adult dolls and grey-haired dolls.

'Does this one look like the bad man, Alex?' one of the detectives asked as he picked up the doll with grey hair. Climbing out of my father's lap, I glanced at the doll curiously.

'No!' I replied confidently. Several weeks had now passed since my mother's death and it was the first time I had been asked anything about what happened that morning.

'Does this one look like the bad man, Alex?' the other asked, as they showed me a doll with black skin.

'No!' I replied once again. The detectives stayed seated on the grass beneath me while I hovered above them with a big smile, occasionally leaning on my father's shoulder. I was enjoying the game.

'What was he wearing, Alex?'

'Was he wearing a T-shirt or a collar shirt?'

As the detectives pointed at their own clothing or that which my father was wearing, I explained to them that the killer had been wearing a white shirt with a collar.

'Blue trousers!' I added suddenly, expanding on the description.

'Jeans?' they asked, pointing at their own.

'Not jeans!'

Somehow, I could remember every single detail with perfect clarity. A few moments later, as we continued the game, I explained to the detectives that the killer hadn't removed any of his clothes. But when I told them that he was wearing a belt over the top of his shirt they were all confused.

'Are you sure, Alex?'

I was adamant. 'Belt over his shirt!' I told them again. This detail was later to be confirmed by adult witnesses who had been present on the Common shortly before and after the attack; and was to underline how accurate my memory of the event really was.

'Did the man who killed Mummy have short hair, like Daddy, or long hair like …?' My father mentioned one of his closest male friends who had a long pony tail.

'Short hair!' I replied.

The detectives were limited to a small number of dolls and were unsure about asking me any more questions. Even so, this was real progress. By the time we left the Heath that morning, I had provided a detailed description of the assailant and the clothes he had been wearing for them to use as the basis for their investigation. He was a fit man with short hair, wearing a white shirt with a collar and buttons, blue trousers that weren't jeans, brown shoes, with a belt over the top of his shirt and a black bag over his shoulder. They could now attempt to corroborate this description by talking to people who had passed close to where my mother and I had been on the Common that morning.

Meanwhile the press, in the absence of hard facts, grasped at straws and printed stories that were wild exaggerations or simply wrong. I had become a 'tragic tot' whom papers claimed would never speak again.

One morning soon after the visit with the detectives, my father and I went back to Hampstead Heath for our daily walk, this time accompanied by my father's friend with the long pony tail. We were soon horsing around, pretending to be trains on a wide open area. At first our friend was wary of playing rough with me, concerned that I might be frightened by someone lunging towards me, but I was having the time of my life. They were both on their hands and knees on the grass, trying to catch me as I ran between them as fast as I could. I was squealing with delight and wanted the game to go on and on.

After some good fun, we sat on a bench under the trees to recover. From our vantage point we could see all the way down the hill and far into the distance. My father and his friend were testing my reading skills, making me identify the letters inscribed on the bench, when all of a sudden, for no apparent reason, I become deeply distressed. My face crumpled and I started feeling the same spasms run through my body as in my nightmares. I was terrified to the point of tears.

'What's wrong, Alex?' my father asked as he lifted me into his arms. He couldn't see any trigger for my extreme change of mood and was becoming deeply concerned. There appeared to be no good reason for my sudden change of state: there were no other people anywhere near us. But, speechless with terror, I pointed down the hill. More than 200 metres away, at the very bottom, a middle-aged man was walking towards us with an Alsatian dog at his side. He was wearing a large overcoat and had a very distinctive crouched-over, lunging walk.

'Is it the man who's frightening you, sweetheart?' my father asked as he buried me in his arms. But I was so scared I could barely speak.

My father assumed that I must be frightened by the man's walk in the same way that children are sometimes frightened by the distorted faces of old people. That this level of terror had been triggered by something as slight as a man all that distance away, whose face we couldn't even see, however, troubled my father. Was this kind of behaviour going to become a part of everyday life? he wondered.

As I peeked down the hill again, I spotted the man with the dog continuing to shuffle in our direction. Even though he was still a long way away, it was clear that eventually he was going to reach us.

'I want him to go away!' I pleaded in tears.

But my father thought that we should stay put and that walking away or heading back to the car might intensify my fears. So instead his friend went trotting down the hill to intercept. When he reached the dog-walker, he told him that a little boy further up on the hill had recently been bitten and was frightened of his dog. At first, the old man was not at all sympathetic and continued walking straight towards us. But when our friend insisted, he eventually turned away and headed off into the distance.

Some time later, passers-by present on the Common on the morning of the attack were to confirm that they had seen a man answering the description I had given the detectives and that this man had a distinctive lunging walk.

My flashbacks to the attack were being triggered at the most random times; manifesting themselves in ways the adults around me struggled to understand.

As my father drove us back to my grandmother's house, I sat in the passenger seat of the car, gazing silently out of the window. Suddenly, I heard our friend in the back seat attempting to open a wrapping as discreetly as he possibly could. Without turning around, I sniffed the air inquisitively. 'I can smell Kit-Kat!' I exclaimed.

'Smart kid!' our friend laughed. 'Can't hide anything from you!'

Several days later, the detectives drove us to visit a child psychologist who lived in a small village north of London. This time, both sets of grandparents came along to offer their support, following closely behind in their respective cars.

As we pulled up outside, I studied the house from the back seat of the unmarked police car.

The psychologist, a grandmotherly figure, showed us all inside. At the back of the house there was a garden with a fish-pond and a little slide on the lawn, with flowerbeds marking the edges. Inside we were invited into a large room filled with toys and child-size furniture. When everyone was seated, the psychologist introduced herself to the group and began to talk about her work. I was busy exploring the objects she had put out on a small table but as always carefully followed the conversation at the same time.

The child psychologist continued by telling my family that child trauma, accidents, violence and death were themes that she was used to dealing with. Although my case was unprecedented, through her work she had touched on similar themes and dealt with children who had been through similar experiences before.

If I was able to talk about what had happened the day my mother was killed, she explained, it would be beneficial for me. Children who had gone through trauma, she believed, could often describe some of what had happened almost straight away – but what they could convey was limited by their vocabulary and understanding of the world. What I had seen and experienced were a serious matter, the outcome of which depended largely on what action was taken. The effects, she said, could not be fully assessed until much later, and I would require ongoing treatment.

Although I had already provided an accurate description of the man who killed my mother, and had done so in just one morning, based on a few simple questions, according to her, it would take me a number of years before I would be able to provide such a description.

The child psychologist proceeded to tell everyone how she had heard about my mother's death through the media. Those poor people! What they must be going through right now, she had thought. In order to put everything into context, she concluded, it was a good idea if every adult in the room explain how they themselves had found out about my mother's death.

I played quietly on the other side of the room, listening intently as my family members shared their story and everyone shed tears, except me.

No one had asked for my opinion, or for me to tell my story. But now the psychologist was walking towards me.

'You were there when the bad man killed your lovely mummy,' she began. 'It's such a dreadful thing to have seen! You must have been so frightened when all this was going on! It's such a terrible thing to have happened to your lovely mummy. And there was nothing you could do about it. You must have felt so small and helpless. You must have felt so angry that you couldn't do anything to help your mummy ...'

I continued playing with the toys on the table but became more and more frantic as she continued.

Why are you telling me this? I wondered. I had been playing peacefully, without disturbing anyone. Now I felt trapped, forced to listen to things I already knew better than anyone and didn't want to hear again.

'But the bad man with the knife was so much bigger than you, and so strong, there was nothing that you could do ...' I only glanced at her face from time to time and was beginning to bang some of the toys against the table. She was intentionally making me relive the events of that day and it was clear to everyone in the room that I was reliving it all inside my head.

'You were so small there was really nothing you could have done, even though you must have wanted to help her and to stop him hurting your lovely mummy!'

The more she went on, the harder I banged things around in an attempt to block out the sound and make her stop. Finally, as my distress reached its peak, I crushed a box of pens and hurled it across the tabletop.

'Look!' she said, pushing a finger doll of a little boy with dark hair into my hand. 'Here's little Alex. And maybe, one day, when you're ready, you might be able to tell us all about what happened to little Alex on that very, very bad day. Your worst day ever ...'

I took the doll, hoping to put an end to her performance. But one thing was certain in my mind; I didn't have the slightest interest in talking to her.

'And I'm sure that he remembers lots about that terrible, terrible day, and the bad man who killed his lovely mummy, because he's such a clever little boy ...'

Another appointment was arranged and everyone said their goodbyes.

On our return, as the detectives drove us back to my grandmother's house, my father took a piece of paper and with one of my felt-tips he began to draw some cartoon figures.

'Alex, was the man who killed Mummy a fat man or a thin man?' he asked, pointing at each figure in turn.

'Thin man!' I said firmly, as I pointed to the drawing.

From the front of the car, the detectives were listening attentively.

'A thin man, like this?' he asked, pointing to the cartoon of the thin man. 'Not a fat man, like that?' he asked, pointing to the fat man.

'Thin man, like that,' I repeated.

My father drew two more thin figures. One had short hair and the other had a pony tail all the way down his back.

'Did the man who killed Mummy have long hair, like this?'

he asked as he pointed to the paper, repeating the question he had already asked me a few days before. 'Or short hair like Daddy or ...' He pointed to one of the detectives' heads.

'Short hair.'

'Are you sure?' he asked. 'Not long hair like ... Mummy?'

'Short hair,' I replied again, adamantly.

I was enjoying my father's game, and although I had already answered all these questions on the Heath, I was happy to answer them again.

'What can I ask him next?' my father asked the detectives, hoping to make the most of the opportunity.

'Big or small?' said one. 'But then again, everyone's big to a child ... It's hard for them to tell the difference.'

'How about hair colour?' suggested the other.

My father looked for colours in my box and drew some more stick figures. There weren't many shades to choose from.

'Alex, did he have yellow hair like Mummy, or black hair like Daddy?'

'Or brown hair?' interjected one of the detectives.

But they weren't the right colours and, with absolute certainty, I said 'no' to all of them and the pens and paper were put away. It had been a long day, I was getting tired and the car ride was coming to an end.

CHAPTER 6

THE FUNERAL

'A sensible man will remember that the eyes may be
confused in two ways – by a change from light to
darkness or from darkness to light; and he will
recognise that the same thing happens to the soul.'

Plato

It was a dark, rainy morning as I sat in the back of one of
several cars driving in a slow procession through the streets
of a small Bedfordshire town. The date was 4 August 1992, and
with my third birthday a week away, we were to attend my
mother's funeral service at a local church. To prepare me for
the event my father had explained to me briefly that it was
going to be a special party for my mother. Until then I had
never stepped inside a church and didn't really know what to
expect. The sombre heaviness of that morning, however, was to
remain deeply imprinted in my mind.

The ceremony was being held primarily for my maternal grandparents who, although not religious people, still needed a formal ritual to mark my mother's departure from this world that might provide them with a sense of closure.

My mother had shared many of the beliefs of the Christian faith, but she wasn't a religious person either and had only rarely attended any church services. What was important for her was that her ashes be placed in a beautiful spot by the few people who meant the most to her, and this had already been arranged.

As we stepped out of the car in front of the grey Victorian church that morning, the hordes of reporters had to be held back by a police cordon so that family and friends could enter the building. We were more than 100 miles away from London, but it seemed that even here there was no room to breathe. In an attempt to protect me from their lenses, my father once again shielded my face as he carried me inside. But as much as he tried to protect me from the repeated invasions of privacy, he knew that he could not do so forever. We were up against a very large and powerful machine.

After the publication of my picture, my grandfather had lodged a complaint with the Press Complaints Council and after considerable effort he had been able to reach the person responsible for the offence. In a private conversation the newspaper editor had admitted that he was sorry for what he had done but insisted that the story was 'just too big to miss'. No penalty, fine or public reprimand was incurred by either the editor or the proprietors of the newspaper in question. Meanwhile the detectives who were handling the investigation into my mother's death had told us that their hands were tied and that, although they now needed my help more than ever before, there was nothing they could do to protect me from exposure.

As my father and I followed my mother's coffin into the church we were seated on one of the pews to the left of the aisle, close to the front, where extra space was left around us. I looked around but there were no signs of the celebration my father had spoken of. The atmosphere was bleak and oppressive, everyone was silent or spoke in whispers and the church was filled to overflowing with strangers I'd never seen before. Some of them I knew, of course – my grandparents, uncles and family friends who loved and cared for my mother – but none of my own friends were there, and there were no other children at all. Everyone looked sad and depressed. In front of the altar, my mother's coffin was set on a stand and flowers carefully placed on top.

The ceremony began with the dark sound of an organ played several rows behind us. My father had brought some Lego for me to play with, but the music was too overpowering, and I was feeling very uncomfortable.

The ordeal seemed never ending. Tense and nervous, I wriggled and fidgeted the whole time as I sat on the hard, wooden bench beside my father. Eventually, however, the organ stopped and I slowly began to relax. Moments later, my maternal grandfather rose from his seat and made his way to the front of the church where he stood, poised and dignified, a brave smile on his face. He had prepared his speech beforehand, and although at times he had to stop as his voice trembled, he managed to retain control and complete his speech with eloquence.

My father had prepared a poem he intended to recite, but as my grandfather finished, my father, choked with tears, signalled to him to read the poem for him instead. Only just managing to hold back his own tears, my grandfather slowly began to read the poignant and beautiful words which had been sent to us by well-wishers, and were written in 1932 by Mary Elizabeth Frye, an American florist.

Do not stand at my grave and weep.
I am not there. I do not sleep.
I am a thousand winds that blow.
I am the diamond glints on snow.
I am the sunlight on ripened grain.
I am the gentle autumn rain.
When you awaken in the morning's hush
I am the swift uplifting rush
Of quiet birds in circled flight.
I am the soft stars that shine at night.
Do not stand at my grave and cry;
I am not there. I did not die.

As my grandfather finished reading the poem and the congregation listened, in absolute silence, I was suddenly captivated by a pair of beautiful butterflies that had, magically, found their way into the church. They fluttered through the beams of light that shone through a stained-glass window, catching everyone's eye as they gracefully lightened the darkness of the day, and the heavy atmosphere that enveloped us all.

* * *

When the ceremony was finally over we climbed back into the car and, worn out by the experience, I immediately fell asleep. When I awoke, I was in my father's arms and we were sitting in another, smaller room, with just my grandparents and uncles.

My mother's coffin was once again at the front of the room, sliding through an opening behind. I watched it disappear, while in the background an organ, a softer one this time, began to play the first few bars of a song my parents often sang me to sleep with.

Even now, whenever I hear it, I am immediately transported back in time and find myself lying peacefully on the sheepskin in my bed, with my mother on one side and my father on the other as they cradle me with, 'Let me wrap you in my warm and tender love', and I drift off into a deep, peaceful sleep filled with beautiful dreams.

The service in the crematorium was a stark contrast to the ceremony we had only just witnessed hours before, and the energy that enveloped us was calm and serene. I stood, relaxed, quietly observing everything that was happening. I instinctively understood that my mother had returned to the essence from which we all come, and I knew, because my father had explained it to me, that this ritual was what she would have wished for.

But it had been a long and emotional day and I was very tired. Maybe it was this, or perhaps it was seeing how important my mother had been to so many people, but that night, despite my usual nightmares, I slept deeply.

The very next morning, printed in all the newspapers, was the inscription on the card which I had carefully placed on my mother's coffin – intended only for her.

'Mummy, you gave me all your being, every moment of your time and always all your love.'

A few days after the funeral, my father and I drove with my mother's parents to my great-grandmother's home, on the Dorset coast, to lay my mother's ashes to rest.

For my mother, it had always been a very special place. Not only had both her parents been to school here, but in her early years she had spent a lot of time with both sets of grandparents, who lived nearby on the coast. Her maternal grandfather had been in the military, working in electronics, and had owned a small motorboat. He had often taken my mother and her brother out on fishing trips or, at night, to watch the fireworks under the stars from out in the bay. My mother had very happy memories of those years, and always recalled what a great time she and my uncle had, playing on the beach for weeks on end, amongst family and friends.

It was here that, on a cliff with a breathtaking view across the sea, we all got down on our hands and knees to dig a hole and carefully place the small jar that contained my mother's ashes. Then, with my bare hands, I covered the jar with earth.

For me, burying my mother's ashes gave everything meaning and for the first time my grandfather, who had managed to hold back his feelings ever since my mother's death, was suddenly overcome with emotion. Nearby, I played contentedly with my grandmother until it was time to leave, happy that a beautiful place like this, exposed to open skies and the power of the sea, would be where the remains of my mother's body would rest.

* * *

After burying my mother's ashes we all stayed on for a few more days. One morning my great-grandmother sat watching me quietly as I stood on the balcony of her front room, gazing out over the beach to the sea, when suddenly an ambulance siren sounded in the distance and I jumped back into the house. My great-grandmother was deeply upset to see the distress on my face. But in an instant I was back to normal, thinking that no one had noticed, and my great-grandmother chose not to say anything.

Later, she would explain to my father that the wail of the siren must have triggered an immediate response in me, reminding me of the morning my mother died.

During this time we made regular trips to my grandparents' house, on a leafy lane in Bedfordshire. I was feeling particularly unhappy one morning, so my father decided to take me to a neighbours' house to see their exotic pets. Their home was filled with iguanas, parrots, guinea pigs, rabbits and – less exotic but equally fascinating – cats and dogs. But as much as I loved seeing them, this time the visit didn't have the desired effect and I returned feeling just as miserable as before.

The very next day we went to visit their neighbours' house once more. This time I was interested only in the rabbits and I stood as close as I could, silently observing them. By the time we got back to my grandparents' house I was crying all over again. My father gave me something to eat and drink, but I was still miserable. Nothing he could do would make me feel any better and I was only becoming more and more distressed.

'It's the rabbit, isn't it?' he asked eventually.

Almost immediately, my crying started to slow down.

'Did it remind you of Mummy, sweetheart?' he asked. 'She promised to get you a rabbit, didn't she?'

I nodded ever so slightly.

My father began to talk about my mother. How much she loved me, how much he missed her, how she would never have wanted to leave us, and what a wonderful mother she was. But, far from cheering me, nearly everything he said made me cry even more.

Eventually, he offered me a biscuit from a tin. There were several varieties and I picked out the one I liked best. But, before I could put it in my mouth, the biscuit crumbled in my hand. When I realised it was the very last one I started crying again.

My father offered me every other kind of biscuit in the tin and then everything else in the house that he could think of but nothing else would do; I wanted *that* biscuit.

It must have been incredibly hard for my father, with his own grief so raw, to be confronted by my seemingly unstoppable tears. Neither of us could have what we most wanted in the world – and so, at that moment, all my anguish was focused on a biscuit. If only I could have that biscuit, the one I most wanted, everything would be better.

And so my father, desperate to stop my tears in any way he could, carried me out into the rain, placed me in the car, strapped me into my seat and drove us into town to the nearest supermarket. Once inside, I looked over the shelves and decided to choose a different packet altogether. I had cried the whole way there, but now I was happy again. But just as we headed to the checkout counter to pay, my father suddenly realised he had come out without any money.

'We've got to go back,' he told me.

I couldn't bear the thought and, forced to return the biscuits to the shelf, burst into tears once again. As I cried my eyes out, my father carried me back out into the rain, strapped me back into my car seat, and drove all the way back to the house, where he pulled me out of my car seat one more time, carried me into the house to find his wallet, and then repeated the whole exercise in reverse until we were finally back at the biscuit stand once again.

When I saw that I was going to get my biscuit after all, my tears instantly stopped. My father paid and put the biscuit into my hand and, for the first time that day, I smiled.

Around this time, my father and I visited a nearby swimming pool one afternoon. Ever since I was a baby my mother had taken me regularly, and I loved the water. What I enjoyed most of all was throwing myself off the side of the pool and into my mother's arms as she stood in the water.

Even though I couldn't quite swim yet on my own I was perfectly happy out of my depth with armbands and spent most of my time in the main pool. On this particular occasion we'd been playing in the water for some while when I began jabbering incoherently and acting as if I could no longer hold myself up.

At first, my father thought it was just a game, but when he reached out to support me I clamped down on his wrist with all my strength and threw my arms around his neck.

'What's wrong, Alex?' he asked. 'What's wrong?'

I stared into his eyes, distressed to the point of tears.

My father was deeply concerned, but still couldn't understand what had triggered such a violent reaction. He looked around the pool and then realised that, based on the description I had been able to give so far, one of the lifeguards bore a strong resemblance to my mother's killer. He also had the same fair hair and the same narrow, fox-like face as the man with the lunging walk whom we had seen walking his dog on Hampstead Heath.

'It's the lifeguard who's frightening you, isn't it?'

'Yes,' I replied, clinging on to him tighter.

'He looks like the man that killed Mummy, doesn't he?'

'Yes.' I squeezed even harder.

'But it's not the man, is it?'

I turned my head to take another look at the lifeguard.

'No,' I replied immediately.

'He's too tall, isn't he?'

'Yes,' I smiled with nervous relief.

Now that I was more relaxed I was able to study him closely from the safety of my father's arms. Not only was the lifeguard much taller than my mother's killer but he had much longer hair. Even though the resemblance between them was striking, I knew that they weren't the same person. To reassure me even more, my father told me that the man responsible would soon be locked in a prison cell, and asked if that would make me happy.

'Yes!' I exclaimed, and within minutes I returned to my games without giving the lifeguard another thought.

After our first visit, the child psychologist's house had been fitted with hidden microphones and concealed cameras. Unlike the extension in my grandmother's house, this time everything had been installed professionally and only a few wires remained unconcealed, behind the sofa.

In the past, children's evidence had to be presented 'live' in court, but by this time a recording of the child's testimony could be included as supplementary evidence. The testimony of children under the age of seven would, however, in most cases, probably not be given any weight as it was considered that they could not distinguish between right and wrong and their memories were not reliable. If and when the time came for a trial to take place, it would be up to the judge to decide whether evidence I supplied could be heard or not.

We returned to the child psychologist's house regularly and each time, as in the first session, I moved around the room searching for relief from her attempts to draw me back to what she called 'my worst ever day' or the 'day you probably don't want to think about at all'. It was clear every time to those present that I was right back in the moment the attack took place.

One day, during such a moment, I began violently stabbing the pencil I had been drawing with into the pieces of paper on the table before me. Deeply upset, my father stepped towards me, trying to intercept and snap me out of my trance. But as I turned to him, I stabbed the pencil towards his face. The pieces of paper lay on the floor, their surface deeply indented with dots.

'I know how much you must remember your worst ever day,' the child psychologist began once again. 'The police are here to catch the bad man who killed your lovely mummy and to put him in prison, where he won't be able to harm anyone else again. Do you remember getting out of the car with Mummy on that terrible day?'

'And Molly was there,' I answered.

'Alex, did you see the knife that the bad man used to kill Mummy?' my father asked.

'Yes,' I replied calmly.

At this, one of the detectives interjected. 'Alex, we're going to show you some knives, so you can tell us which one it looked like.'

The detective placed a tray on the children's table in front of me. There was some ordinary household cutlery, a bread knife, several large kitchen knives, a penknife and a hunting knife.

I instantly picked out the hunting knife.

Later, it would be confirmed that the blade matched the shape of the weapon as established by the pathologist who had examined my mother's wounds.

'What did the bad man do after he had killed Mummy?' one of the detectives asked.

'The bad man washed the blood off in the water.'

Although every bit of information I revealed was another piece of the jigsaw, the process being used was becoming arduous and upsetting, for me and for my father. He was beginning to feel concerned and could no longer see any value in terms of my recovery. He thought that we were spending too much time doing the police's job for them, and as the sessions went on he began to be troubled by the possibility that, rather than being therapeutic, they were actually impeding my recovery.

The child psychologist appeared relentless and, as she told me how 'terrible' it was and how 'terrible I must have felt', every time my playing got louder and louder, until it was a strain to make out what anyone was saying. Over and again I would bang and bash the toys around the room as hard as I could in my attempt to drown her out.

Very early on, she had told my father that noise generation was typical of all children she worked with, and that on the tape recordings of her sessions you could always hear the crescendo rise when she persuaded the child to relive the most 'scarring' events of their lives. Unsurprisingly, it was in the midst of the moment of greatest distress that the noise became the loudest. During these moments, I would look at my father in complete confusion, searching for help and asking him, without words, why he was letting her cause me such pain.

Even though he was told that knowledge and understanding of how to work with child witnesses had evolved greatly, my father was increasingly unsure of the emotional toll this heavy-handed approach might take and he struggled every time to resist the urge to just pick me up and take me away. How much more of this could I bear? he wondered.

However, no one could tell how much information I might possess that could be useful to the investigation, and so it was agreed that the sessions would have to continue.

Meanwhile, the police had asked my grandfather if he would agree to talk to the press again. They were desperately looking for new avenues and ways to generate new leads and considered that with his participation their chances of success would be significantly increased.

At first my grandfather was extremely reluctant. After his experience with the media so far, he had no desire whatsoever to deal with them again. But, determined to do all he could to prevent the assailant from harming anyone else, in the end, he agreed.

The police informed him that the interview would take place at New Scotland Yard, and that in order to make the process as easy as possible for him there would only be one journalist and one television crew present. The interview would then be freely distributed to all news agencies, newspapers and TV channels, in an attempt to raise as much public awareness as possible. They hoped that someone, somewhere, would come through with another piece of the puzzle.

With the promised safeguards in place, my grandfather made the trip to New Scotland Yard and put himself through the gruelling process of talking about his daughter's death once again. But the very next day his interview was made public, appearing in one newspaper alone, along with the colour photographs that had been lent to the police to help with the investigation. Now they had been leaked, and EXCLUSIVE was printed at the top of every page. Betrayed once again, my grandfather was furious. He couldn't bear to think that people might believe he had sold our family pictures to the gutter press.

CHAPTER 7

THE PRESSURE COOKER

'If you do not change direction, you may end up
where you are heading.'

Lao Tzu

M y father and I were struggling to build a new foundation together, and our lives were out of balance. After so much time spent in the company of police, detectives, psychologists and grieving relatives, my father was determined to re-institute some childlike fun into my life and to make sure that my birthday, due almost four weeks after my mother's death, did not just pass us by.

The eleventh of August fell on a Tuesday. My grandparents were holding a family party the following weekend, but on the day it was just my father and me, and he decided to take me to a wildlife park outside the city to mark the occasion. So early that morning, mindful that we weren't being followed by the press, we headed off in our old grey Volvo estate.

During the drive, I sat in the passenger's seat quietly gazing out of the window. After pulling up in the car park we climbed onto a bus that took us through a large area surrounded by forest where all types of exotic animals were kept in large enclosures. We saw tigers, lions, black panthers, chimpanzees, penguins, deer and, in a darkened area, nocturnal animals like lemurs and lorises.

When we came to the leopard enclosure I was immediately transfixed by the sight of a magnificent male, making its way down from the branch of a large tree and parading majestically right in front of us. As I watched silently, my father told me the story of White Eagle.

Legend had it that a Native American called White Eagle had married into the family, several generations back. Just how White Eagle arrived in Africa a century ago is something of a mystery, but the story goes that he was a great hunter who had been recruited to accompany an expedition. So in love did he fall with the majestic beauty of the African continent that when his task was completed he decided not to return to his homeland, but stay and build a new life there. Later, during the course of his travels, he married into the family and settled down in Zimbabwe, with his new wife, for the rest of his days.

Years later, when he was already fairly elderly, he was walking through the bush one day when a leopard suddenly dropped onto him from a tree. He was badly wounded, but White Eagle managed to survive, killing the leopard with his bare hands. Soon, however, he became seriously ill from the poison inside his bloodstream that emanated from the rotting meat that sticks behind the claws of large cats. A couple of years later White

Eagle passed away, but the legend surrounding his name was to be passed down through the family for generations to come. The story was always told with great pride and everyone liked to believe that they had inherited the bravery and strength of our illustrious ancestor.

I loved the story, and watched the leopard with awe, imagining how strong White Eagle must have been to kill one of these powerful creatures.

Moments later the skies darkened. A storm was approaching, but there was just time for me to have a ride on a pony called Miguel before it began to rain heavily. Afterwards, we ate our sandwiches in the car while thunder rumbled and lightning flashed all around us. I was having a great time, and when the skies cleared we went back outside to look at some more animals.

Soon after my birthday, my father, aware that after weeks spent with adults I needed to get back to playing with children my own age, made a list of all my old friends from nursery and one by one asked me whether I wanted to see them.

'Do you want to see …?' he asked, naming a little girl who had come to visit us a few days before.

'Yes,' I replied, without looking up as I played with my toys.

'Do you want to see …?' He mentioned the daughter of a friend of my parents.

'Yes.'

One by one my father went through the entire list and I answered 'yes' to all except one boy.

'Do you want to see …?'

'No,' I answered, still without looking up.

When I first befriended this boy, my mother was delighted because, until then, all the children I got on best with were girls, most of them just a little bit older than me and keen to take me under their wing. My father could only assume then that the reason I didn't want to see this particular boy must simply be because I preferred girls. But a thought suddenly flashed into his head. Most of the girls I played with were brought by their mothers, but this boy always came with his father.

'Are you afraid of ...?' my father asked, naming the little boy's father.

'Yes,' I replied, still without looking up.

'Did the man who killed Mummy look like ...?' He named the boy's father again.

'Yes.'

'Do you think it was ...?'

'Yes,' I said, still without looking up as I continued to play with my toys.

My father was startled and at a loss for words. Surely it must be that the boy's father looked like the killer? Either way, for him, it was entirely understandable that I didn't want to see anybody who even vaguely resembled the person who killed my mother.

He didn't ask me anything further, but later in the afternoon, at the child psychologist's house and out of my earshot, my father explained to the detectives the conversation we had shared earlier that morning. They hung on his every word.

'In light of how the investigation is progressing, that is very interesting,' one of them said. 'Did you notice Alex's reaction the day you went to lay the rose on the Common?' asked the other. After escaping the barrage of press photographers, and just as we reached the safety of the police car, the father of this same boy had approached us. My father, with me still in his arms, had stopped briefly to accept his condolences before climbing into the car.

'Alex looked like he was wriggling out of your arms to get away …'

'No,' my father replied, confused. He had assumed that it was the press I was anxious to escape from.

In most murder cases the killer is someone known to the victim, rather than a total stranger. And, in the absence of other leads, it seemed that my friend's father was already of interest to the police, not only because he resembled my description of the killer, but because his alibi relied solely on the word of his wife.

In the days to come, the idea of the boy's father being responsible would eat away at my father. With a lack of concrete evidence to incriminate him, the police could not arrest him, and it seemed to my father that the investigation appeared to be going nowhere. In the late hours the thought of taking matters into his own hands consumed him to the extent that late one night he telephoned the boy's father.

'Hello?' the man replied. But my father didn't utter a word and after several silent seconds he hung up.

My father was under tremendous pressure from all sides. Besieged by the police, the press and well-wishers, desperately short of sleep and trying to manage his own grief, his priority was to care for and protect me. He felt that I would never be really safe until the killer was behind bars, but a month after the attack the investigation was floundering, and the thought of taking matters into his own hands repeatedly flashed through his mind.

The press had, inevitably, discovered where we were. And once they did, life became even more oppressive; we couldn't leave the house without running the gamut of reporters and photographers who waited outside my grandmother's gate from dusk until dawn and followed us everywhere we went, so in order to escape the constraints of the life we were living we travelled out of the city as often as possible. We were constantly on the move, slipping out in the early morning to drive to the countryside where, for a few hours, we could feel something close to normal again.

One day we drove down to the south coast to stay with my father's best friend out in the countryside, and my youngest uncle, Chan, decided to join us. Far from the big city, it was an ideal place simply to potter around as my mother had so loved to do.

As long as I had my sheepskin and my blankets, I was always perfectly happy to travel anywhere my father took me, providing we were together. I still needed to have him with me from the very first moment of the day until I closed my eyes at night.

No one else could take his place, even for a few minutes. It was my father who had to watch my morning cartoons with me and make my breakfast. When he went to take a shower I would follow him to the bathroom. 'When are you going to be finished?' I would demand to know. And, though it was exhausting for him, I refused to allow him to leave my side.

Sometimes this meant getting into the water and pulling him out physically. I didn't care in the slightest if my clothes got wet and he had to change them all again. But the morning after we arrived on the south coast I was having so much fun playing with my uncle and our friend that my father managed to have his first bath in peace since my mother passed away.

I'd brought my pens and paper with me and, as there were lots of exciting things to provide inspiration, I happily sat on the floor drawing. Before long there were sheets of paper scattered all across the tiles. 'Mummy would have liked these!' I told our friend, proudly. I was having a great time, and the neighbours even brought a cake for me. In the backyard there were cows wandering around and Molly jumped the gate, attempting to chase them. Miscalculating her leap she caught herself on the top bar and gashed her stomach. Luckily it wasn't too serious, and with a bit of rest we knew she would be fine.

Later that day we drove down to the beach. It was grey and cold when we arrived, but my father decided to take a swim. As always I wanted him to stay and play with me, so I attached myself to his leg. Unperturbed, he carried on all the way down to the water's edge, where I eventually let go. Taking one look at the grey, churning waves, I decided that, rather than getting wet and cold, this time I'd stay on the beach.

'Come back!' I called after him as he headed out to sea. But ignoring my call, he kept going, and realising that this time he wasn't coming back I set off back up the beach to rejoin the game with our friend and my uncle. At moments like this, knowing I was safe with people I could trust, my father was able to spend a few precious minutes alone, and I began to see that I could manage without him, if only for a short while.

During our stay, we also went to visit an aquarium. As well as the usual tanks of multicoloured fish lining the walls there was a film show on display in a side room. In the film, a blonde woman was feeding bait to sharks. There was a lot of blood and swirling water and the young woman appeared and disappeared from the screen.

My father and I were the only spectators. He only stayed for a few minutes before rejoining our friend and my uncle among the fish tanks. But I was fascinated and wanted to stay, so I sat on my own and watched for a few minutes at a time before leaving to check that my father and the others were nearby. A few minutes later I would wander back in to watch a little more of the action until eventually I had seen the film all the way through. I was having the time of my life and came away with a plastic shark's head on a stick, with a mouth that opened and closed when I squeezed the handle. I used it as the baddie in all my games for weeks to come.

Back at my grandmother June's house I watched my first feature film, *E.T.* Sitting on my father's lap, I talked in his ear the whole way through. I wanted to know all the details. What's an alien? What's he doing? Where's he going? When's he coming back? What are the children doing? Why's he hiding in the cupboard? And on and on and on.

But when I saw that E.T. had died, I went suddenly quiet and stopped asking questions, transfixed by what was happening to him and the children's efforts to revive him. When, after a long and tense wait, the enchanting creature came back to life I felt extremely relieved and began asking questions all over again – until finally the film ended, the alien flew home, and I burst into tears.

'I want to see him again!' I wailed, as part of me was immediately transported back to the morning on the Common.

The following weekend, my birthday party was held at my mother's parents' home, with my uncles and both sets of grandparents. Out in the garden, I played happily with my uncles, while the adults prepared a barbecue and chatted amongst themselves.

In addition to the cards and presents from family and friends, a room at Wimbledon police station was overflowing with letters and gifts sent to me by well-wishers from all over the country. Heaps of toys had arrived from people moved by what happened. For several weeks, as the story remained in the headlines, I had been the most famous child in Britain, and the public had responded warmly.

My father knew I had quite enough toys of my own, and after some thought he decided to donate them to charity. But we kept a couple of teddy bears and all the books to look at together and bit by bit we read through all the letters. They'd come from people of all ages and backgrounds. A mother wrote to explain how her little boy of around the same age came down the stairs one day to find her crying. When he asked why, she explained what had happened to my mother and me. The little boy went running straight back upstairs and came down again with his favourite teddy bear. 'Send it to him,' he said.

An elderly lady in her eighties had written from Scotland enclosing a postal order for a few pounds that she had taken out of her pension. There was even a card from the remand wing of a well-known prison, wishing me luck. To my father it was a stark reminder of the reception awaiting whoever was eventually to be convicted.

* * *

'Alex, do you know the name of the man who killed your mummy?'

I had been listening to this question for hours. This time it wasn't my father asking the questions, nor the child psychologist, but one of the detectives. I had recently visited his home and played with his daughters, who were around the same age as me.

'Alex, do you know the name of the man who killed your mummy?'

'The bad man!' I replied every time. A name they had first assigned to the assailant themselves. Sometimes I came close to the detective and looked into his eyes, as if to provoke him into asking the same question again. It had become a game.

'Do you know the name of the man who killed your mummy, Alex?'

'The bad man!' I replied once again. Without my knowing, the police were focusing on the father of my friend, hoping that I would name him and they would catch it on camera. But I simply played the game.

'You know that these big detectives are there to catch the bad man,' the child psychologist cut in. 'And you know that anything you tell them helps them with their job.'

I remained silent.

'It's all right, Alex,' my father said softly. 'You can tell every-one what you've told me ...'

I had never given my father a name. I had only answered 'yes' when he'd asked me if I thought the boy's father killed my mother. Although I knew his name, this was a different question altogether.

'Do you know the name of the man who killed your mummy, Alex?' the detective asked for the hundredth time.

'I think he likes you too much,' my father interjected. 'I don't think he's convinced that you're tough enough to deal with this monster … You've got to do something to impress him. Haven't you got handcuffs, or something?'

The detectives explained to me that as well as the two of them there were lots of other policemen and that they had handcuffs, truncheons, police cars and vans, as well as cells with thick steel doors with huge locks to imprison the 'bad man' – so he could never escape. But still I was not impressed and continued to remain silent.

At last, my father turned to me. 'Alex, I'm going to write the name of the person that you told me on this piece of paper … and you, because you are such a big boy, you can read it out to the detective!'

I couldn't yet read. I could tell the shapes of some letters of the alphabet, but wasn't yet able to spell out words. Picking up the piece of paper, I began walking towards the detective, but when I was almost there I turned back towards my father. Encouraged by the look in his eyes, yet feeling hesitant and uncertain, I pronounced the name of the boy's father out loud. Not because he was the bad man, but because I had been persuaded to say it. I realised in that moment that I'd been tricked. Another element of trust had been lost.

The detectives, however, thought that we were getting somewhere and within a few days they came up with a new incentive: to take me to see a real, locked cell door for myself.

As we made our way down a narrow staircase into a dark corridor lit by overhead strip lighting, with cells lining each side, I stood beside my father, filled with excitement and curiosity. One of the detectives encouraged me to see for myself just how secure the doors really were. At first I was hesitant but after a little encouragement I edged forward cautiously and touched one of the heavy doors. To me it was a game, and for a moment I glanced back at my father with a big grin. But suddenly a man lurched forward out of the shadows, scaring the life out of me. Muttering some muffled sounds, he reached out, attempting to grab me. The detectives rushed to my aid and, throwing him back into the cell, they slammed the heavy door, which had mistakenly been left unlocked.

They were mortified. 'That was close!' one of them said under his breath. 'That could have gone really wrong ...' said the other, as they bustled us away.

Minutes later we were taken to another block underneath the police station where, as we stood in front of one of the empty cells, the detectives once again slammed the heavy metal door shut and told me it would be impossible for the 'bad man' ever to escape. But by then I was badly shaken, and no longer interested in their games. I held on to my father's hand and wanted to leave. I wasn't even interested when they took us to see the police horses, in an effort to cheer me up.

A few days later, my father received a message from senior officers. They wanted him to hand me over to the child psychologist so she could take me back to the Common on her own, accompanied only by the police.

My father thought they were completely mad. There was no way he was going to allow this to happen. His scepticism about the psychologist was growing every day. We had been attending appointments at her house for more than eight weeks and all we were doing was going over the same old ground again and again. In the meantime people's lives were in danger, and in order to cooperate, in the end, my father agreed to take me back to the Common himself.

The police were keen to discover any new detail, no matter how small, and their hope was that my return would prompt some new recollection. So on a damp morning in mid-September my father and I left my grandmother's house and made our way across town in our old Volvo.

During the journey, I gazed silently through the window. All my father had told me was that we were going for a walk on the Common. He'd been worried about explaining why we were going and wanted me to have as little time as possible to dwell on the subject.

We pulled up on a quiet street behind Wimbledon police station. All of a sudden the child psychologist and the two detectives climbed in the back. I was caught off guard; this wasn't at all what I was expecting. The child psychologist immediately began pushing my father to explain. Everyone began talking to me at the same time, saying that I was there to help the police and that they wanted me to show them the way I had walked with my mother on the morning of the attack.

For the rest of the drive I sat silently, with a bad feeling about the situation unfolding.

As we pulled up in the car park on the Common, I could see regular police cars, unmarked cars and officers in uniform and plain clothes, making their way towards us.

My father turned off the ignition and the child psychologist and the detectives climbed out of the car. He unbuckled me from my seat and I jumped onto his lap. The air was filled with tension, strangers were surrounding the car, everybody wanted something from me, and I didn't like it.

My father explained to me that we were there to help the police, and that we wouldn't be long, but as soon as he opened the door I gripped the steering wheel with all my strength. When we visited the Common only days after my mother's death to leave the flower for her I had been eager to return, but this time it felt completely different and I didn't want to go. My father tried to pull me away from the wheel, but I held on tightly and wouldn't let go. This was exactly the kind of reaction he had expected from me the previous time and he was beginning to question whether the visit was a good idea at all.

But as strongly as I was holding on to the steering wheel I wasn't breaking down, and he assumed that if I was truly scared I'd be kicking and screaming. Uncertain, but concluding that what I needed was the reassurance that if I let go of the steering wheel and came out of the car everything would be all right, he pulled my hands off the steering wheel and lifted me out of the car.

As he carried me in his arms, he began walking along the path that I followed with my mother that morning. The child psychologist and the two detectives followed, while officers flitted in front and behind.

Soon I stopped crying and wanted to get down and walk beside my father. When we passed the spot where we buried Birdie, officers I didn't know were calling out to me, 'Which way did you go next, Alex?' I could hear lots of voices, all firing questions at the same time, so that I could hardly hear my father above them.

But despite everything, I remained calm. When we reached the mound, all I wanted to do was climb to the top and run down again and again. 'Were you going this way with Mummy that morning, Alex?' my father asked, pointing down the slope. 'Were you going to the pond?'

But I was now more interested in the blackberries beginning to appear in the brambles. The vegetation had changed, everything had grown over the last couple of months and it was hard to recognise our trail.

Eventually I led everyone all the way down to the pond and we began to head back up the hill again and make our way under the canopy of trees. With the undergrowth almost reaching my face I could hardly see.

'Which way did you go, Alex?' officers called out, as they pointed in different directions and headed off to explore the bushes nearby. We were close to the spot. 'Which way did you go, Alex?' someone called out again. At that moment, as I struggled to negotiate a ditch, I slipped and fell over. Picking myself up from the ground, I saw blood running down my grazed leg and let out a loud wail.

By now my father was fuming. *Why have I done this to him?* he asked himself. Whatever this expedition was, whatever the child psychologist and the police hoped to achieve by bringing me back to the Common, it had to end. Lifting me up into his arms, and ignoring everyone's cries, he started running back towards the car as fast as he could.

As we emerged from the trees he tried to go even faster but at that moment I spotted some beautiful blackberries and wanted to stop and pick them. I tugged at him and began to cry even louder. We stopped for a moment and I stood on one leg, my face covered in tears as I stuffed my mouth with as many blackberries as I could.

Shaking with emotion, my father was anxious to get away. We were only a couple of hundred metres from the car park, but the pack was close behind. Pulling a handful of fruit off the bush, he scooped me up and hurried to the car.

Just as he managed to shove me into my seat and strap me in, the child psychologist appeared with one of the detectives, shouting at us through the window, the rest of the pack close behind them. Starting up the engine as fast as he could, he pressed his foot down on the accelerator and the tyres skidded in the gravel as we drove off at full speed.

'Don't drive so fast!' I wailed as I began to cry all over again.

Minutes later we pulled up in the car park of a nearby tennis club, overlooking a large cricket field.

By then I had already stopped crying but as my father turned off the engine he burst into tears himself.

I sat quietly on my seat, studying his face and glancing out of the window.

'I'm hungry,' I said.

My father reached down under the seat and pulled a yoghurt out of a bag, handing it to me with a spoon.

I took a couple of mouthfuls. 'Why did you drive so fast?' I asked.

'I'm sorry,' he said.

I took another mouthful. 'You frightened me.'

'I'm sorry. I didn't mean to frighten you,' he said, wiping away his tears. 'I won't do it again.'

I recognised the park outside. My mother and I had once been there for a stroll together when we'd accompanied my father to a tennis tournament at the club. I wanted to get out and play; at least for the moment, I'd forgotten the cut on my leg and the ordeal we'd just been through.

But my father was close to breaking point. He knew we couldn't live like this for much longer. We were stuck in a nightmare and something had to change.

CHAPTER 8

END OF THE BEGINNING

'Who wishes to fight must first count the cost.'

Sun Tzu

In late September I walked with my father along the seafront of a small village on the French coast. Over two months had passed since the attack on the Common and, seeking some kind of release from the suffocating intensity of our lives in London, we had recently arrived for a three-week break. The season was over, the summer crowds had all left and on deserted streets the shutters lining the empty houses were pulled down night and day. But what looked like a ghost town would serve as the perfect hideaway from the pressures at home.

Days before our departure, my friend's father had been ruled out of contention and a new suspect had come into the picture. On 17 September the police had arranged for the

BBC's *Crimewatch* programme to present an identikit picture of my mother's assailant, based on my description. The response had been immediate. A man living close to Wimbledon Common, named Colin Stagg, had been identified by several callers.

The Operation Edzell team, which had been set up to investigate my mother's murder, already had him in their sights. He had been on the Common, walking his dog, on the morning my mother was attacked, and earlier in the year he had been accused by a woman of indecent exposure on the Common. He claimed that he had been sunbathing nude and she had simply come across him, but after taking his solicitor's advice to plead guilty he had been fined £200.

The police had called in clinical psychologist Paul Britton, who drew up a profile of the killer. He concluded that whoever murdered my mother would be a male in his twenties or thirties, probably living on his own, not far from the Common, quite possibly interested in the occult and knives, and prone to sadistic sexual fantasies.

The day after the broadcast Colin Stagg had been arrested and his flat searched. No direct evidence had been found, but the team considered their suspicions confirmed when the search turned up books on the occult, an altar, some gloves and a sheath knife.

Over a period of three days he was questioned by detectives of the Edzell team and, under the guidance of Paul Britton, shown selected pictures of the crime scene in an attempt to provoke a confession.

During the interviews, he admitted to walking his dog on the Common the morning my mother was killed, but claimed that he was at home when the attack took place, even though he had no alibi to back this up. He also denied owning a white shirt, and although none was found during the search of his flat, several witnesses claimed that he had been wearing one at a recent funeral.

At no time during the interrogation did Colin Stagg admit to the killing of my mother, and since the evidence was at best flimsy he was released without charge.

The evening of his release, a female witness, who had been followed by the assailant minutes before my mother was attacked, made a call to the police. During Colin Stagg's detainment she had already picked him out at an identity parade, and after watching footage of him on the news leaving Wimbledon police station and seeing his distinctive loping walk, she was more convinced than ever that he was the man responsible for my mother's death.

Colin Stagg's distinctive walk tied in with my own description of the assailant and the Edzell team concluded that it was a statistical impossibility for someone else with the same walk, and fitting the same description, to have been present on Wimbledon Common that morning. They were now considering asking me to attend an identity parade from behind one-way glass. But even if I were to pick Colin Stagg out, they had no material evidence on which to base a case.

While the drama raged back at home, almost 1,000 miles away, in the second row of houses off the seafront, we found a brick bungalow to rent with a couple of rooms and a small garden. Apart from the wide, empty beach, the seafront, and a small marina nearby, there was nothing much to see, but here we could be out in the open in peace.

Justine, my mother's childhood friend, had flown out with us and her younger brother joined us a few days after our arrival. Their parents were originally from France and they had both been born nearby. Having them with us was a great help, and by sharing the driving and cooking, my father was able to relax for the first time in months.

The first days of our stay had been stormy and while the beach was buffeted by howling winds and rain we were forced to stay inside. My father began making up some children's stories and I spent happy hours helping him to create drawings to go along with them.

Eventually the weather calmed and the sun began to shine. We swam in the sea several times, but the water was already cold, so most of our time was spent playing on the beach instead. After the storm I collected bits of driftwood washed up on the shore, where I found 'hosepipe sticks', 'sword sticks', 'hammer sticks' and 'socket-wrench sticks', which kept me amused for hours as I handed them out to my father and our friends, telling them exactly how they had to play with them.

On the water's edge we built large sand dinosaurs together, collected sea shells to take back to the house, and in the garden we collected snails to make them race along the tracks we built for them. One of my favourite discoveries, however, was an old car tyre that I spotted washed up on the shore. For days I found endless amusement rolling it up and down the beach from one end to the other.

My father spoke a reasonable amount of French, picked up while hitchhiking around France to play in tennis tournaments when he was younger. I, however, was not at all interested in replying to the strangers who stopped to say, *'Bonjour!'* I would glare at them with my arms crossed and a sulky look on my face. But as soon as they left, and no one was looking, I would practise repeating the unusual sounds I was hearing around me every day.

The peace and quiet, the anonymity of France, the time spent with each other, these were the things my father and I needed more than anything else. Life in London had become impossible. I would forever be under the microscope, everyone knowing everything about my past, my life heavy with the expectations of what I might or might not become.

A few weeks before our departure, my father had received a letter from old friends he had lost contact with, suggesting that our two families meet. For some time he had been trying to encourage me to play with children my own age so he was eager to make the most of the opportunity. Not only did they live very close to my grandmother's house in North London but they now had four children of their own, the youngest of whom was born only days before me.

One afternoon we drove over to their house and parked on the opposite side of the street. My father had explained to me that these were his friends and that they had a boy my age that I could play with, but I wasn't at all happy with his plan. As soon as he unbuckled my seatbelt, I grabbed the steering wheel again and wouldn't let go. Even when the boy appeared in the doorway next to his mother, I continued to hang on with all my strength. It was some time before I finally let go and allowed my father to carry me into their large Victorian house.

At first I was cautious and wary of the boy's mother and older brothers, but eventually I decided to get down from my father's lap and play. The connection between us was instantaneous, and Isaac and I were soon inseparable. I had never had so much fun playing with another child. In no time we were spending almost every day together. Whenever one of our games slowed down, one of us would immediately think of something new and we'd be off again, running around the house from morning until evening before collapsing with exhaustion at bedtime.

Isaac had experienced many physical challenges in his young life and was often strapped to a ventilator to help ease his breathing difficulties. In his few years of life he had almost died several times. His brothers and sisters were all strong and his mother had to pay special attention to him. He needed to rest more than I did, so in between our play sessions my father would drive around until I fell asleep. Afterwards, we would return for more play until dinnertime.

If I was ever in trouble, Isaac would immediately spring to my defence. 'He didn't mean it,' he would say, always doing his best to protect me. Such was the case when we were playing around one afternoon and I threw a pair of scissors at him. Luckily I missed, but there had been witnesses and everyone was deeply upset. I was told off in no uncertain terms by my father and made to apologise.

It was a watershed moment which I have never forgotten, and although it was undoubtedly appropriate for my father to correct me for what I had done, perhaps for the first time I became aware of how much I was under the microscope. Ever since my mother's death my behaviour had been immediately judged and categorised by everyone present. If I did something 'naughty' that any other child might have done, it was because I was 'traumatised' and a danger to everyone.

Isaac and I were soon playing happily again but it wasn't long before another game provoked my father's concern once more. 'You're not allowed to play with those!' he snapped one day when I came meandering down the stairs with a plastic knife in my hand. My mother had never given me toy weapons and my father intended to keep it that way. But as much as I enjoyed my father's approval, I was still determined to get away with anything I thought was fun, even if he didn't like it. And so I continued to play with whatever toys I wanted when he wasn't looking. When I was eventually caught with the same plastic knife, my father immediately snatched it from my hands all over again and all I could do was regret that I hadn't been more careful to hide it from him.

Observing the situation, Isaac's mother tried to explain to my father that perhaps he was in danger of making things worse than they actually were. After raising four children of her own, she had been forced to let go of many idealistic concepts along the way. 'Maybe he's just playing,' she concluded. She continued by telling the story of a little boy who had been invited to a party at their house who wasn't allowed sweets at home. As soon as he came through the door and saw all the goodies at the birthday party he went completely berserk, proceeding to devour everything in sight.

'If you really believe he shouldn't have these things, then maybe you shouldn't bring him,' she concluded. Even though it was hard for my father to accept, he could see her point. He relented, and from then on I was allowed to play with any of their toys that I liked.

The idea of playing with toy knives might not have been a concern for Isaac's mother, but it wasn't long before another game was to leave her absorbed in thought. One weekend we went to the Heath with Isaac's family for a game of trains. As usual, I was soon directing things. Isaac was an engine, like me, and he was allowed to run around wherever he liked, as long as he came back from time to time. But I decided that his mother would be a carriage and would not be allowed to leave the station without me.

Every now and then I would interrupt my running around and come back to collect her. The two of us would then chuff around until it was time for me to take her back to the station and leave her once again. I instructed her firmly that she was to stay right there and I kept my eye on her at all times. If she tried to move I would shout for her to stay where I'd left her. But what seemed like just an innocent game struck her as significant. She was a blonde woman who I felt wasn't safe without me watching her.

When the press had carried the picture exposing my face, my father had cut my hair in an effort to make me less recognisable, and as we were now living the other side of town Isaac's mother offered to drive us to their hairdresser for a fresh cut one morning. When the young woman in the salon brought the scissors towards my face, I did everything I could to force my way out of the chair, making it impossible for her to finish the job. But as I showed no obvious distress, those present thought I was just being rebellious. My father, however, could see that the act of a stranger bringing sharp instruments towards my face had disturbed me deeply, and he decided that from then on he would be the only one to cut my hair, at least until I was old enough to decide for myself.

With all the concerns about my well-being and our life under the spotlight in London, it was an enormous relief for both of us to spend those three weeks in peace, on the French coast. As we stood together on the deserted beach, gazing silently out to the sea, it was as if we had been magically transported to a different world, and all the tensions of our life in London lay far behind us. It was our first taste of life away from the pressure-cooker environment of home and my father was becoming convinced that we would have a far brighter future there than we ever would in the UK. Besides which, he and my mother had never truly wanted me to grow up in a city. Together they had dreamed of a place just like this. They loved the wildness of France, with its endless open skies.

Perhaps there could still be a home for us here, my father thought, knowing that my mother would have loved the idea, and would be with us in spirit. Perhaps we could find a village school somewhere where nobody knew about our past. With a little luck, my father would find a way to teach tennis, as he had already done many times before. What was more, my mother's parents loved the beauty of France as well; they had even been looking for a second home here just the year before. The only concern was the language barrier I would inevitably be faced with.

One night, soon after our return to London, my grandmother June walked past my bedroom and heard me crying. She rushed in to find me out of my bed, huddled in the corner of the room. Tears were streaming down my face and I was whimpering in fear. My eyes were open and I appeared to be tracking something across the room, but when my grandmother spoke to me I didn't respond.

She went running to call my father, who saw that she was as white as a sheet, and the two of them came rushing to see what was wrong. Even after my father had picked me up I didn't respond. I was in a deep, somnambulistic state – apparently awake but still sleeping, my eyes fixed upon something moving around us.

Eventually I began to relax, and when my father finally put me in my bed again I fell back into a deep sleep. In reality, I had never been truly awake. Over the days that followed, nightmares of a similar nature returned with a vengeance and were to recur every night. They didn't appear to have any direct relation to the attack, but I was constantly experiencing images of violence and terror, which could only be the result of what I had witnessed.

One of my recurring nightmares involved finding myself in ancient Egypt, and being thrown into a deep pit overflowing with snakes. It wouldn't be until years later that I would learn to jump off tall cliffs, precipices and bridges in my dreams, descending gently through the air only to wake, every time, just before reaching the ground. Some refer to this as lucid dreaming, but to me these experiences would only serve to underline the many layers of what we call 'reality' and inculcate a strong belief in the afterlife.

After repeatedly finding me out of my bed, huddling fearfully in the corner of the room, my father became deeply troubled. He decided that we needed to set aside regular time to talk about my mother and what had happened, even if it was only for a couple of sentences a day. Perhaps if we talked together it might allow my fears to dissipate and allow me to sleep peacefully for the first time in months.

I was still playing almost daily with Isaac, and his mother eventually suggested to my father that I might be ready to start going to nursery again. The one Isaac attended, she explained, was fantastic. It had been open for more than thirty years and Isaac's older brother had also been there and had loved it too. The owner was a survivor of a Second World War German concentration camp and still wore her prison number tattooed inside her wrist. Because she had not had any of her own, she had dedicated herself instead to the nurturing and care of generations of young children.

My father thought it would be a good idea. The advice the psychologist had offered at the hospital months before still rang true, and by sending me to nursery every morning not only would we be building a solid routine, but I would be able to spend even more time playing with Isaac.

I settled in with surprising ease, and was soon attending every weekday morning. The nursery formed part of yet another large Victorian home typical of suburban North London, where it occupied the entire ground floor, the basement and the garden behind. Inside there was a child-size kitchen which I especially enjoyed. Preparing pretend meals for my parents had always been a favourite game of mine.

After all the time spent in the company of policemen, psychologists and grieving relatives, it was a welcome return to some kind of normality. I was with children my own age, in the care of safe and kind adults, and while I was there I could forget about everything going on outside.

But our lives were still under the microscope and even at nursery there was no escape from the prying lenses of the press. Every morning we had to push past journalists waiting at our garden gate and, once they'd discovered where I was, they camped in the gardens near the nursery to photograph me as I played. And no matter how happy I appeared to be with my new friends during the day, at night I was still terrorised in my dreams and my father had to come running as I screamed like a tortured animal.

Perhaps it was the straw that broke the camel's back. But after the unrelenting intrusion from the press and the police, my father's mind was made up once and for all when a detective informed him that the police had been contacted by a Sunday newspaper, insisting that if he refused to comply with their request for an exclusive interview, they would run a story stating that he had found new happiness with a 'mystery blonde'. As it turned out, the mystery blonde was the mother of my best friend.

That this kind of behaviour was possible and that my father was being informed of the scheme by the police, who were doing nothing to prevent it, proved to him that we would not be free from this kind of intrusion until we left the UK. We had the choice of staying behind and fighting, or we could go somewhere far away and start a new life.

And so at the beginning of 1993 my father announced to our family that we would soon be leaving the country. His decision caused a great deal of controversy and upset.

My mother's father decided to stop talking to him and her mother told him that he was causing them a second bereavement. It was abnormal, she said, to want to take a small child away from his native country and run away deep into the countryside.

Their fear of losing contact with their only grandson, so soon after the loss of their daughter, was understandable, but my father's main concern was my well-being. As a single parent, he was determined to bring me up in the way that he thought best for my peace of mind and my future.

One night in early February, when the press who routinely patrolled the house had finally left, my father woke me from a deep sleep. His face was serious. 'It's time to go,' he announced.

It had been over seven months since my mother's death, and for the last few days he had been preparing bags with clothing and other belongings, which stood piled up in the hallway close to the front door. As we made our way down the darkened staircase I was still barely awake. Outside in the freezing cold, I helped him squeeze the last of our possessions into the trunk before he strapped me into my car seat, wrapped me in a blanket and we drove off into the night.

For some time I had known that we were going on a journey, but now, with Molly left behind, a night that had begun like any other offered little clue as to how much our life was about to change. From my seat in our old Volvo I gazed out the window into the darkness.

'Where are we going?' I wondered intently to myself.

CHAPTER 9

INTO THE UNKNOWN

'The holy land is everywhere.'

Black Elk

The trip on the ferry was stormy and wavy and I felt dizzy and sick. Sitting in a large, empty dining hall, I watched the dishes sliding from side to side across the table top. Outside it was a dark morning and as the boat rocked heavily with every new barrage of waves, the rain hammered against the deck.

From our table we could just about see through the steamy windows, but it was too dangerous to walk on deck and all the doors had been locked. Behind us was England and ahead of us France, but for now we were caught between two worlds: the past and the future.

My grandmother June and Gordon, my father's friend with the pony tail, had followed us in a second car with the rest of our belongings and would be joining us for the next part of the journey.

'Why are we leaving?' I asked my father as we made our way off the ferry. He explained that we were going where the weather was warmer, and that the further we drove the warmer it was going to be. I would now be able to play outside all year round.

During the drive it continued to pour. I gazed out of the window from time to time while I played with my toys and the music sounded gently through the car speakers. For most of the journey I hardly spoke a word. At one point my father reached across to find that my legs were icy cold. The ventilator had been stuck open with outside air blowing through and I hadn't even complained. My mind was somewhere else.

We reached Paris and passed through without stopping, driving on as morning became afternoon and afternoon became dusk. I dozed off intermittently, lulled by the motion of the car, but by the time darkness fell everyone else had been awake for over thirty-six hours and they were all exhausted. That night we slept in a roadside hotel.

The next morning we resumed our journey. The drive seemed endless, and they were long, uncomfortable hours for everyone, but eventually we made a stop on the outskirts of a small town to take a break. Through the window I could see a climbing frame and a slide, but when I stepped out of the car the ground was frozen hard, the toys were covered in ice, and it was impossible for me to play.

As the first flakes began to fall we found a restaurant for lunch, and by the time we returned to the car park the cars were covered in snow. After clearing the windows we climbed back inside, coaxed the engines into life once more and resumed our journey.

With the snow masking our tracks it was a struggle for my grandmother to follow our trail. In the days before mobile phones it was easy to get separated and lost, so we were constantly on the lookout, making sure that everyone stayed within sight.

We drove on through the afternoon, eventually leaving the snow behind us, and at sunset we pulled into a small town close to the sea. Here we met up with a young doctor and her husband who were friends of friends back in England. They lead us across the fields to a small country hotel, which was to be our home for the next few weeks.

We hadn't eaten for hours and it was getting late. The village was all but closed down for the night but, much to our delight, a phone call made by our new friends meant that the pizza oven of a local restaurant would be opened specially for us.

After a delicious feast, we strolled back to the hotel through the frosty country air for a warm, snug night of undisturbed sleep. The next day, after unpacking all our belongings from their car, we hugged my grandmother and Gordon goodbye and waved to them as they drove off into the distance. It was now just the two of us.

For the next few weeks it continued to snow heavily and we were unable to be outside for long. My father said that as soon as the weather changed we could go out and look for a house to live in, but in the meantime driving was treacherous. So, apart from visiting our new doctor friend and her husband a couple of times, we were locked up together in our room, playing with my toys or watching TV in a language I didn't yet understand.

Finding things for me to eat was also problematic. The locals couldn't understand why anyone in their right mind would force their child to be vegetarian and there was very little served in the restaurants and cafés without meat. On more than one occasion, when my father explained to the waiters that I didn't eat meat and requested something vegetarian, they nodded in agreement, only to return five minutes later with a carefully prepared ham sandwich.

On one of our rare outings to the surrounding villages to look for a house, the car broke down in the middle of a snow-storm and my father climbed out to look under the bonnet.

'Why aren't we going?' I asked, as soon as he clambered back in.

'I can't get the car started,' he replied, just about managing to hold himself together as his patience was tested to the limit. After several more tries the engine finally fired up and we were underway once again, although it was certainly not the last time that our old Volvo was to break down at crucial moments.

As we drove back to the hotel night fell upon us. Along the country lanes we saw cars crashed into roadside ditches, and my father couldn't help but comment on how fast everyone around us was driving. Later we laughed together watching the drivers of snow-bound vehicles interviewed on the news, declaring, 'On n'allait pas vite!' We weren't going fast!

'I was playing sword-fighting when the bad man came!' I told my father as we fenced with washed-up sticks on the beach one morning. Though it was still bitterly cold, we had managed to escape from the hotel for a few hours. It was the first time in months that I had volunteered a comment about the attack. 'He pushed me into the mud! That wasn't nice!'

My father paused. He wanted to make the most of the moment, to encourage me to express everything that was on my mind. 'Where were you when the bad man was hurting Mummy?' he asked.

'I was with Mummy,' I replied, beaming. 'Why does the bad man like you?' I asked as we continued to play, wondering why he hadn't been killed as well.

My father was dumbfounded by my question. 'He doesn't like me. He's afraid of me! He would never have attacked Mummy when I was there. He knew what I would have done to him.'

'He had a bag,' I added.

'What did he have in the bag?'

'The knife,' I replied, as we walked further down the beach. 'If Thunderbirds were around they would catch him!' I added cheerfully.

'Where did the man come from?'

I signalled to my right. 'I saw him. Mummy saw him. It was black, I think …' I carried on, referring to the bag. Suddenly, I became angry. 'He pushed me over!'

That night, while I was asleep, my father wrote down everything I had told him.

As the snow thawed we were able to explore further afield, and after weeks of constant driving back and forth our quest for a new home was finally over. At last we had found the right place and were able to move out of the hotel. We were both over-joyed. We had seen countless places and this one, near Montpellier, we agreed, was by far the best.

The old stone house formed part of a farm building and looked out over a large courtyard where dogs I was eager to befriend wandered freely and tractors were loaded and unloaded next to the machinery which was stored next door.

At one end of the courtyard there were chicken runs and across from our front step, behind a high stone wall, lay the wine cellars with their pungent smell of fermenting grapes. Here we would be surrounded by vineyards and beautiful, wide-open spaces. Even the locals were fond of the house and thought it to be the kind that would be ideal for artists and musicians.

When we arrived, the place was completely unfurnished. My father had brought along the bed he shared with my mother and after unpacking it from the boot and putting it together we set off to a nearby town to pick up a few things. There we found a bed on stilts for me, a fridge and a washing machine, and our doctor friend and her husband loaned us a cooker. Although it would be a while before it truly felt like home, for the moment we had all we needed.

The local village was almost a kilometre away and our nearest neighbours were two farm workers and their families who lived next door above the tractors. Beyond the stone wall and the wine cellars stood a handsome country house where the owners lived with their two teenage children.

Even though the farm workers and their families were suspicious of a man who chose to stay at home to look after a small child, from the very beginning they were always generous and welcoming towards us, offering eggs from their chickens and vegetables from their allotments. The owners allowed us to take wine produced on the property directly from the vats and, at mealtimes, my father would pour a drop into my water. As the seasons unfolded around us we would discover that the branches of the nearby trees overflowed with figs, almonds, cherries and apricots. My favourites, however, were the tiny, sour blackberries that appeared in the summertime and proved much rarer and harder to find.

As the weather improved we could begin to make the most of our beautiful surroundings and I soon made friends with Remy and Audrey, two children exactly the same age as me whose fathers worked together in the fields every day. Much of our time would be spent playing in the yard or running wild through the fields. My new friends were perfectly happy with me not speaking their language, and Audrey, who had an instant crush on me, would talk away for hours, firing out words like a machine gun. I couldn't understand a thing, but she would look upon me indulgently, as if I was just a little bit slow.

As much as I enjoyed playing with my new friends, because of red tape I wouldn't be admitted into the local village school that they attended until the following September, and in the meantime, for my father and me, life settled into a new pattern as we set about decorating and furnishing our new home.

Weeks after our arrival, the house was still almost completely empty and, with bare walls and only an old diesel boiler, the damp that came up from the stone floor made the old farm building cold and inhospitable. And so my father and I set out early every morning in our old Volvo to the nearest town, searching through the aisles and shelves of large DIY stores and hypermarkets for cheap furnishing ideas, cleaning products, paint, tools and any other bits and pieces we might need.

The winter days were still short so we would head back to the house as fast as we could to get on with finishing whatever tasks were at hand before it became too dark.

For the first time since my mother's death, I had my own room again with my own special things. Together we painted the walls blue and cut stencils from the cardboard of cereal packets so that I could have Thunderbird rockets flying around me as I played. In the evening, before I fell asleep, my father would sing to me until I drifted off – but even in our new home nightmares still haunted me every night.

The endless journeys back and forth from the nearest town in search of furniture eventually became tiresome and my father decided to build whatever furniture we needed himself. We were alone every day and without the support structure we'd become accustomed to in London he was busier than ever, so as a consequence I now received far less attention. For the greater part of the day I would amuse myself on my own, as he set about completing the carpentry work and, in order to get the job finished, he became much firmer with me. If I asked for anything, he would often snap back at me, insisting that I wait. For better or for worse, our underlying frustrations at finding ourselves isolated in the depths of the countryside without my mother soon began to surface and direct themselves towards each other.

Since my mother's death, my diet had become limited as a result of living in other people's houses. Now that we had a kitchen to ourselves again, my father started searching through my mother's recipe books, attempting to produce different dishes. But food connected me intimately to her and I wanted my meals exactly the way she prepared them for me. My mother never gave omelettes to me, and when my father began preparing them with the fresh eggs from our neighbours, I immediately gagged and vomited onto my plate. There was no way I could force the eggs down and I received the worst of my father's anger as he shouted in frustration and threw plates at the wall.

My mother didn't believe in hitting children, if at all avoidable. She had never shouted or smacked me, and was always intuitive enough to come up with more effective solutions while remaining calm and in control. Normally, if we were playing in the bedroom and an incident arose, she would take one of my favourite toys and put it on a shelf I couldn't reach until I calmed down. If this wasn't enough, she would put me out in the hall alone and close the door behind her, all the while holding the door shut and telling me that I was welcome to come back in as soon as I was prepared to behave myself. I had the whole house for myself, but would throw myself at the door with all my strength, trying to open it. Eventually, however, I would get tired and worn down – and would have no choice but to surrender.

But with all the pressures he now found himself under, my father wasn't always able to remain calm. At times he would go berserk, shouting and chasing me around the house with a slipper.

But these tactics never worked. I was strong-willed and could stand getting smacked if that was what was needed to win the power struggle. I would not give in, especially if I felt justified in my cause. Our worst confrontations were nearly always centred around food as I thought it was extremely unfair to be forced to eat things that made me sick.

In a way, I was pleased when my father snapped because it showed he had lost control. I also knew that, when he cooled down, he'd feel bad about his behaviour and try to make peace.

What I didn't know at the time was how much these situations would eat away at him. He didn't want me to grow up alone with a bitter father, as he had done. But despite his best efforts, he feared that, in many ways, the pattern was being repeated.

Until the age of nine, my father had lived alone with his mother. Her own mother died when she was a baby, and her father, an RAF pilot, was on active service, flying Lancasters and dropping bombs on the Germans during the Second World War. As a consequence, he was forced to give up his children for adoption and they all went to different families.

My grandmother's new parents never explained her origins. Instead, one day when she was 12 years old, a neighbour unintentionally let slip that she was adopted. The revealing of a foundation built on deceit brought her great confusion and distress. She wouldn't find out who her biological parents were until many years later, when she would eventually reunite with her father and long-lost siblings.

Meanwhile, my paternal grandfather was born in Cape Town and grew up in Zimbabwe. He would often tell tales of his colourful childhood, growing up with his pet chameleon under blue skies and playing with his many brothers and sisters beneath the fruit trees. When he was small, his mother passed away and his father remarried. His new stepmother had many children of her own; together, they were enough to field a complete football team and they often played matches against their neighbours, who also had a very large family.

Although all the children were highly educated, my grandfather and his siblings received second-class treatment, while the children of his new stepmother enjoyed most of the first-class attention. From his later beliefs and views on life, it seems clear that not enough love and nurturing had trickled down to him.

When it was time for him to leave school he went to study in South Africa, and although he might have wanted to be an engineer or a doctor, under the oppressive system of apartheid in which black people were second-class citizens in their own land he was only allowed to study a trade, so by default rather than choice he decided upon mechanics, and in the late 1950s he moved to England, where he was to meet my grandmother.

At that time, signs for 'Whites Only' could still be seen across the UK too, but ironically, my grandfather still had greater freedom there than he did in his homeland, and at last he could finally study whatever he liked. Eventually he was to become a schoolteacher, specialising in technical subjects like metalworking and carpentry.

When my grandmother gave birth to my father she was barely more than 20, and my grandfather, who was much older, struggled to leave behind his bachelor lifestyle and adapt to his new role. In my father's earliest memories, he recalls him only as an occasional presence. Later on there would be scheduled visits every weekend, although he would often be handed on to a third party to be cared for.

When my father was six years old he was molested by a stranger in a cinema. Not feeling cherished by those around him, he was unable to confide in anyone and would keep this to himself until he was an adult.

When he was nine, my grandparents swapped over the lease on the flat. My grandmother moved out and my grandfather moved in. My father was deeply affected by her leaving, although at the time all he said was, 'I don't care, as long as I can keep my dog.' My grandmother promised him that he could, but within a few months with my grandfather the dog was gone as well.

Soon after moving into the flat, my grandfather tore up all the carpets and they lived on bare, splintery boards. He said that he was going to fix the floor, but somehow never got around to it. A harbinger of things to come, it was a pattern of starting things and not seeing them through that would remain constant throughout my father's childhood.

Over the following years my father spent a great deal of time on his own, feeling extremely lonely. Although his father introduced him to tennis, as his interest developed into a passion he paid little attention and gave him no support.

My grandmother eventually remarried and he saw her one weekend in four. With her new husband she was soon to have my two uncles, and even though my father got along well with them it was difficult for everyone to integrate together as a family.

'She always wanted to marry a rich man,' my grandfather would let drop from time to time.

'Your father's the tightest man I've ever met,' my grandmother commented in turn, and now that my father was alone with my grandfather for the first time he heard constantly repeated a whole litany of beliefs that only served to demonstrate my grandfather's view of life as a constant struggle: 'Money doesn't grow on trees', 'It's easy for him', 'Seven good years are always followed by seven bad', 'The first million is the hardest', 'Life is like juggling plates in a circus – and there never seem to be enough hands.'

My grandfather always made it clear to my father that life had been far better in Zimbabwe than it was in London, and that the only reason they hadn't already moved was due to the unstable political situation at the time. Even so, one Christmas he promised to take my father there on holiday to see the lions. At the last moment the holiday was postponed until Easter, and when Easter arrived the holiday was postponed once again until summer. And so the story went for several years.

When my father first asked when they would be going, he was answered pleasantly, with further promises. But as time went on his enquiries were met with a withering look and a scathing tone of voice, which seemed to say, 'How dare you ask?'

As the years went on, my father increasingly refrained from asking my grandfather anything, and at the age of 17 he left home to travel the world, playing tennis. Their relationship had never been resolved and it had now been many years since they had even spoken.

My father had hoped, from the start, that my childhood would be different: loving and secure, with two parents who adored one another. He had wanted to give me brothers and sisters and for me to be surrounded by a growing pack.

Bringing me up without my mother was lonely and hard for him. After putting me to bed at night, he dwelt for hours on how tough he had been on me that day. Years later he would tell me that he had thought I must hate him.

But I loved him. If he ever hurt himself I went running to stroke the finger he had cut. In a strange way my father began to feel positively cherished. The fact that I still loved and believed in him gave him the strength he needed to keep going. He attempted as best he could to provide a warm and happy environment for us in our new home, but he was emotionally exhausted and deep in grief. With no back-up whatsoever, he was forced to work through his own demons while continuing to look after me as best he could at the same time.

CHAPTER 10

THE SCHOOL PSYCHIATRIST

'Do not speak of evil, for it creates curiosity
in the hearts of the young.'

Native American Lakota proverb

Although conditions were basic and at night it was bitterly cold, with the old stone house in order we now had two spare rooms to welcome guests, and over the following months we received our first visits from family and friends.

In March, shortly before Easter, my grandmother June and my uncle Mohan came over to stay for a few days, bringing Molly along with them. It was a magical night when the car pulled up in our courtyard under the light of a full moon. We were in the wilds of the countryside and our city dog emerged from the car terrified by the sounds and smells which had her turning in circles. We'd missed her cheerful presence, and having her back filled the house with life, as what remained of our pack was reunited once again.

The next day I set about showing my family my new world. We strolled along the canal, walked the banks of the river and explored the endless vineyards that surrounded our home. I was delighted to see them. But as much as I enjoyed my time with them, I had never been the kind of child who missed people when they were out of sight. I just took things in my stride and enjoyed being with them whenever they were around. The few short days we shared together soon flew by, and this time, as my grandmother and my uncle drove off into the distance, it was three of us watching them go.

Shortly after their visit, and in spite of the rift that had taken place before our departure, my father invited my mother's parents out to stay with us. They drove down for a few days' visit and decided to stay in a nearby hotel. As always, I was happy to see them and, just as with my father's relatives, I was eager to show them around. During their stay, they acknowledged that life for me would have been impossible in the UK and that my father's decision to move to France had been the right one.

Molly adapted rapidly to her country life. She loved running free in the yard every day with all the other dogs. The beach was only twenty minutes away by car and with her for company I began to swim in the sea. I was already a fair swimmer, and even though the water was numbingly cold I loved it. Molly was my lifeguard. She would sit on the breakwater, surveying my every move and whining with concern. When her patience was finally exhausted, she would launch herself into the water and attempt to rescue me by grabbing my neck as if I was her naughty puppy. But she always scratched me with her sharp claws, so in time I had to learn to hold onto her neck and tail as she pulled me back to the shore.

When the Easter holidays arrived, Isaac and his family called to let us know they were driving down from London. Ever since our departure they had been sending workbooks and toys in the post to keep me amused and, just like my uncles, they recorded videos of my favourite cartoons and posted them to me every week without fail.

Unable to go outside, I waited impatiently for their arrival, staring out through the windows for hours on end as the rain sheeted down off the roof onto the flooded courtyard below. As if by magic, the rain stopped just in time, and when Isaac's family finally arrived I couldn't wait to show them all my favourite places. One day, we drove to a nearby river which was known for its dangerous rapids and fast-flowing water. While we paddled around in the calmer eddies, Molly couldn't resist the temptation and dived in after a passing duck. All of a sudden she was caught by the current and quickly carried away out of sight.

Isaac's mother was horrified. After losing my mother she didn't want me to lose my dog as well. Confident that Molly had learnt the lessons that a country dog needed to survive, I carried on splashing about without the slightest concern. But with no sign of her returning, we all climbed into their car and set off down the bumpy dirt road that followed the river's course.

Eventually, we spotted her, as she was washed up onto the riverbank several miles away. Struggling to regain her balance and looking half-drowned, Molly shook herself hard.

'See!' I exclaimed proudly to everyone, as she made her way unsteadily back to the car. 'She's a good swimmer!'

* * *

Easter fell in early April that year and as April gave way to May the bitter winds and snows that had welcomed us to France melted away and suddenly spring was alive all around us. The fields overflowed with new life, green shoots appeared across the vines and wild flowers blossomed on the grass verges. The sun was strong during the day and the house was no longer icy cold at night.

Ever since our arrival my father and I had spent almost every day at home together, but with the start of a new season he decided that I should attend a nursery in a nearby village so that I'd be ready for school in September. By then I'd be four, and he wanted me to get to know other local children and to improve my French.

I didn't like it. Every morning I threw a huge tantrum and hurled myself at the door every time my father turned to leave. On my very first day, a little boy welcomed me by latching on and attempting to wrestle me to the ground. Other boys were continuously punching and kicking at each other, venting their pent-up aggression – but I could see that, in his particular case, it was just his way of showing affection. And so, as he continued to latch on to me every morning, every morning I would push him off again.

The nursery was immaculate, with a large garden surrounded by an old stone wall and a warm, welcoming group of teachers and helpers. But I was a year older than everyone else and found all the games and activities very boring compared to my nursery in London. For two months, until the summer break, I sat on my own every day, and although I reluctantly joined in with the compulsory group activities, in every free moment I isolated myself from the other children and played on my own instead. I would only tolerate the company of the adults and refused to speak any French whatsoever.

My father never let on to me how concerned he was about my behaviour, and hoped that in time I would begin to enjoy being there. From the very beginning, he had decided to keep our background a secret from the staff. He wanted us to have a fresh start and feared that if anyone knew who we were word might get out and the press track us down.

Despite my dislike of nursery, I was happy amusing myself with Molly at home, and continued to play with Remy and Audrey who lived above the tractors whenever I could.

As much as I loved our dog, one day I asked my father if next time around I could have a horse instead.

'Where's it going to live?' he asked.

'In the house with us, like Molly,' I replied.

He was often amused at my childlike logic, and attempted to write down the most memorable phrases I came up with.

'Father Christmas wouldn't like that,' he scolded me one evening when I was being naughty. 'He can see what you're up to.'

'The curtains are closed,' I replied.

'Don't let me see you hit him again,' he snapped when he found out I'd been rough and tumbling with another boy in the yard.

'You didn't see me,' I pointed out.

But not all my phrases were so amusing.

'If anything happens to you, who will look after me?' I asked him in a thoughtful moment, while I sat at the table waiting for my lunch one day.

* * *

With the summer holidays on the horizon, my father wanted to record all that I had recently shared with him that could help with the police's investigation. So one sunny afternoon we sat down at my small table with a video camera set up in order to tape our conversation. This time I explained to him not only the direction which the killer had come from but also that, after he had left, I had picked up a piece of paper and placed it carefully on my mother's body. At the time I thought it was money that had fallen out of her pocket. But in reality it was a receipt from a cash machine. Up until then the police had been puzzled by this detail and concluded that the killer must have left it there for some significant reason.

My father sent the video, via our relatives, to the detectives handling the case. They asked if they could come out and visit us, but my father told them it was out of the question. He was determined not to give away any clues as to where we were.

Soon the tastes, scents and adventures of our first summer arrived, and I spent the greater part of my time playing with a new group of friends that included the little boy from nursery who always wanted to wrestle with me. As the days went by I began to throw out a few French phrases here and there. I acted cool, as though it was no big deal, but inside I was very happy with my achievement. In the beginning, when my father spoke in long sentences with other adults, I couldn't understand a word. But one afternoon he was busy discussing plans for the weekend with some friends as I played nearby.

'I don't want to do that tomorrow!' I exclaimed adamantly, as soon as he'd finished.

Not long after, I made the decision that from then on I was going to watch my cartoons in French. I didn't understand everything that was going on at first, but I watched them every morning all throughout the summer, picking up more and more phrases each day.

That summer I also met my first love. Laure was the god-daughter of one of our new friends and lived in a small town on the coast with her younger brother and sister. At weekends, however, they often came to stay with family near to where we lived.

Laure was beautiful and although she was seven years older than me she had found me very exotic from the moment our eyes first met. The connection between us was immediate. She was very feminine, nurturing and attentive.

Over the following winters we would go on endless skiing and walking trips in the mountains together with her younger brother and sister, visiting old castles and museums when warmer days arrived. Laure loved to paint and draw, so on our return we often made sketches of the places and things that we'd seen together. Whenever we were apart she would write and send me letters without fail, which I loved to collect from the post box in the courtyard, across from our front door.

One starry midsummer night we trekked up to a high mountain plateau surrounded by waterfalls for an open-air performance of *A Thousand and One Arabian Nights*. The show was spectacular. Laure and I watched together, captivated by the horses, camels and knights with raised swords that came running through the audience. After the show, we trekked back hand in hand under the starlight.

When we are alone I asked Laure to wait for me until I was

16, as I would then be old enough to marry her and we could be together, just the two of us.

'Who knows what the future will bring,' she replied with a smile, as she held me tenderly in her arms. 'For now, we should take things one day at a time.'

Towards the end of summer, while walking out in the fields with Molly, under a wide-open sky, my father explained to me that the man responsible for my mother's death had been caught and was being held behind bars. Rather than imposing on me a conversation I might not want, he casually left it open for me to ask any questions I might have. But I wasn't at all interested and didn't even reply.

For me, life had moved on and a new chapter had begun. After all the hours spent in the company of child psychologists and police detectives, I found the subject tedious and unappealing. Since our departure from the UK, I hadn't asked my father a single question about what had happened to my mother or the assailant.

I was still happy to talk about my mother, and would bring her up in our conversations from time to time. One of my most treasured possessions was a bottle of her perfume, Coco by Chanel, which I carefully kept in a chest of drawers beside my bed. I would smell it proudly every now and then and immediately feel her presence enveloping me. The investigation, however, held little significance for me; after all, nothing could bring my mother back, and I was more interested in enjoying my day.

* * *

A few weeks later, a British detective flew out to a nearby town and my father drove to the airport to meet him. The police were now convinced that if and when the case came to trial my testimony would be crucial. If I said what I had already said before – that the killer wore a white shirt with a belt over the top, blue trousers, dark shoes, and carried a black bag with a knife inside – the jury would have enough evidence to bring about a conviction of anyone charged.

'The problem is,' the detective explained, 'the case will never reach trial without Alex. If we're to have a chance at a conviction, we need him to cooperate.' The detective requested that my father sign a document which guaranteed that he would bring me back to the UK to give evidence at a trial expected to take place in the autumn of the following year.

My father had very little time in which to weigh up whether this experience was going to be positive or detrimental in terms of my recovery. My nightmares had slowly begun to recede, but recently he had once again found me, in the middle of the night, huddling in the corner of the room. Tears streamed down my face and I was whimpering in fear.

As before, my eyes were open all the while and I appeared to be following something across the room.

'Do you remember what you dreamed about last night?' my father had asked me on one of these occasions, while I was eating breakfast the following morning, seemingly without a care in the world.

I stared at him, as if insulted by the question. 'No,' I replied.

'Are you sure?'

'I didn't have any dreams,' I insisted.

But even if I didn't talk about my nightmares and awoke as if nothing had ever happened, my father knew they were still there, and so whether or not to allow me to give evidence was one of the most critical decisions he had been faced with. Justice for my mother and, most importantly, other people's safety was paramount to him – but would this affect my well-being? Reassured that there would be no face-to-face meeting with the killer, and that I would be allowed to give evidence via a video link in a separate room, in the end my father signed the document. Ultimately, he knew that living in another jurisdiction there was little they could do to force me to appear if he later changed his mind.

The holidays soon flew by, and when September arrived I began to attend school in our own village. I was now with Remy and Audrey as well as children of my own age once again. But I still wouldn't speak to adults, and from the very beginning my new teacher was concerned. She said that I seemed to understand everything, but that I wouldn't utter a single word to her. Eventually she called my father in for a talk, and told him that I needed to see the school psychiatrist, and that even though I was joining in with all the activities she thought I must be suffering from some form of mental deficiency as I appeared to be learning French so slowly.

Although deeply upset at first, my father saw my teacher's concern more as a vague threat than a definite intention to act, and decided to let the days pass. He knew me well and could see that her upset probably had more to do with the fact that her attempts to coax me into speaking French had all been unsuccessful. He knew as well that for months his own attempts had also been fruitless, but reassured himself that he had over-heard me talking in short snippets to other children throughout the summer, out of earshot of any adults. I had never liked being told what to do, and had made up my mind that I was going to wait until I was ready to speak. In the meantime, my father hoped that my teacher's threats wouldn't be followed up and that he wouldn't have to reveal any of our family background.

For weeks, he had been promising me that we would go skiing when the first snow fell. But just before the trip my temperature rose sharply and he was concerned that the exer-tion might be too much for me. In the end we went ahead with the trip anyway and, to my father's relief, I made an instant recovery and had the time of my life, zooming up and down the slopes all day long. By the time we arrived home I was feel-ing a million dollars.

'This is not the same child!' people exclaimed after I greeted them cheerfully in French for the first time and chatted away with everyone I met. I could now switch seamlessly from one language to the other in mid-sentence and my teacher no longer felt any need to call in the school psychiatrist. In fact, I was talking in such long, complicated sentences that she soon began congratu-lating herself on her teaching skills instead. She even began to complain that I talked so much that I was making her deaf.

But despite my teacher's new-found delight in my improve-ment, an incident soon arose in the school bathrooms which had her questioning my mental capacities all over again.

'Alex has been found in the bathroom passed out, and hang-ing from a towel,' she reported to my father with great concern when he arrived to collect me after school one day.

Alarmed at first, he soon spotted me playing with a group of classmates nearby and could see that I appeared to be absolutely fine. 'Boys will be boys!' he thought to himself. But my teacher was deeply upset. Due to my irresponsible behaviour she said that she would be forced to change the towel system for the whole school.

Earlier that day I had been scolded and punished in front of all my classmates, and as soon as we reached home my father took me to task all over again. Along with the scissor incident with Isaac I remember this as one of the biggest scoldings I ever received. In my eyes, not only had my teacher's description of the event been somewhat exaggerated but it was only because my timing had been unfortunate that she had found out about anything at all.

The truth of the matter was that I had simply been caught red-handed sticking my head through a roller towel and pulling funny faces.

In the end, I had also taken the blame for all the other children with whom I had been laughing and fooling around minutes before, who had all been smart enough to go running through the door as soon as the teacher on duty appeared.

But things soon turned around again when I was invited to the school across the road to read stories in English to a large crowd of older children. From the top of a small stage I stood looking down on them as I recited the passages passionately and enthusiastically and, according to my teacher, put on a great performance. She described me as *'une bête de scène'* – a beast of the stage – and from then on my visits to their school became regular.

* * *

A few weeks later my father was informed that the police in the UK would no longer be requiring my evidence at the trial. The detectives were positive that the suspect they held on remand was the man responsible for my mother's murder and they were confident of obtaining a conviction based on information gathered through an undercover operation that had taken place in the months leading up to his arrest. The evidence they now possessed, they claimed, was far more compelling than anything I could possibly present.

It was a huge relief to my father that I would not be needed, and that, despite the absence of any forensic evidence or confession, the police seemed so certain of their case.

We had now been living in our secret hideaway deep in the French countryside for long enough to watch the seasons change and reach our second summer. Life was opening up for me; I was taller, stronger and could speak two languages. I no longer made my way every morning to my father's bed and my nightmares were fewer and fewer.

The summer holidays soon flew by and when September arrived I was back at school as just another little French boy. But, once again, a dark cloud was gathering overhead.

CHAPTER 11

THE SUSPECT

'Everything that we see is a shadow cast by that
which we do not see.'

Martin Luther King, Jr

'There is too much black in what Alexander draws for me,'
my new teacher told my father as she met him in the
school car park one morning. 'It worries me.' She paused. 'I
want to refer him to the school's psychiatrist. Could you give
me the details of your doctor?'

'The kid's already seen enough psychiatrists!' my father
snapped back unthinkingly.

My teacher stared at him in shock. Without uttering a word,
she turned on her heel and stormed away.

The last thing in the world my father wanted was for me to
be placed in the hands of another so-called professional. He had
heard enough about the 'sick child syndrome' in which children

undergoing continuous treatment of any kind would inevitably end up believing there was something inherently wrong with them.

It was the beginning of autumn 1994 and, aged five, I had recently returned to school for the start of my second year. While we were walking out in the fields with Molly one morning, my father explained to me that the man responsible for my mother's death had just been released from jail. As he had done before, rather than imposing upon me a conversation I might not want to have, he left it open for me to follow up or ask any questions I might have. But once again I remained unmoved and uninterested, and as Molly ran up and down the field nearby, we set off on our trail once again without uttering another word.

Earlier in the week he had received a phone call from my mother's father while I was at school. The trial of Colin Stagg, the suspect the police held on remand, had collapsed at London's Old Bailey in a storm of controversy and media frenzy. The judge assigned, Mr Justice Ognall, had dismissed all the evidence presented by the police.

Ever since his arrest, following the release of the identikit picture only weeks before our move to France, the police had been convinced that Colin Stagg was their man. It was a statistical impossibility, they claimed, for two people fitting the same description, with the same distinctive lunging walk, to have been present on the Common that morning. So convinced were they that, despite the lack of any direct evidence linking him to my mother's murder, the Operation Edzell team decided to try to trap him into a confession and had submitted a proposal to the police Special Operations Unit to mount an undercover, 'honeytrap' operation against him.

In the months that followed, the operation had been analysed and approved by senior officers Detective Chief Inspector Giles, Commander Ramm and the Metropolitan Police Solicitors Department and on 19 January 1993 it had begun in earnest.

The idea was to use an attractive undercover female police officer under the pseudonym of 'Lizzie James' as bait, with the aim of tempting the suspect, a man with a limited sexual past, into a confession. Paul Britton, the criminal psychologist assigned to the case, helped draw up a letter in which 'Lizzie James' explained that she was a friend of a woman the suspect had previously contacted through a lonely hearts column and was looking for a man with whom to share her violent fantasies. It took only two days for Colin Stagg to take the bait, and a correspondence between them began when he replied to her message on 21 January. Soon the two were exchanging letters, graduating over time to long phone conversations in which, at the behest of her superiors, 'Lizzie James' attempted to provoke a confession.

Throughout the process Paul Britton analysed Colin Stagg's letters and phone calls and advised the Edzell team on how best 'Lizzie James' should respond. All in all, 16 letters were sent, purportedly from her, resulting in 27 replies from the suspect. Paul Britton also advised on the production of a tape in which 'Lizzie James' voiced a violent sexual fantasy. The tape was sent to Colin Stagg in June 1993.

Months into the operation and without the suspect ever admitting to my mother's murder, the team had stepped up their attempts to coax him into a confession. In a telephone conversation, recorded by the police and later released to an inquiry, 'Lizzie James' told Colin Stagg how she enjoyed hurting people. 'If only you had done the Wimbledon Common murder,' she said, 'if only you'd killed her, it would be all right ...' But Colin Stagg's only reply was, 'I'm terribly sorry, but I didn't.'

Throughout the operation, the Crown Prosecution Service, the government service empowered to bring a police investigation to court, was regularly apprised of the operation. In addition, four formal meetings took place between CPS lawyers, amongst them Mr Pickston and Mr Hodgetts of the CPS, and senior police officers Superintendent Basset, Chief Inspector Wickerson and Inspector Pedder of the Edzell team.

As the operation progressed, a total of four face-to-face meetings took place in public, and there was discussion of a chain-mail suit being made for 'Lizzie James' to wear under her clothes to prevent an attack if the couple were to meet in a more secluded spot, but ultimately it was considered too great a risk for her safety to continue any further.

The correspondence between them came to a natural end when a genuine lonely hearts writer contacted Colin Stagg through the column and his interest in 'Lizzie James' faltered.

The operation had lasted over seven months and Colin Stagg had not admitted at any time to my mother's murder.

Ultimately, the CPS lawyers concluded that there was insufficient evidence to bring about a conviction against him. Yet, on 17 August, only days after my fourth birthday, the police decided to ignore the advice of the CPS and Colin Stagg was arrested and charged with my mother's murder. Following his arrest his flat was examined minutely and the garden dug up in the hope of uncovering the murder weapon. Nothing was found.

My father had passed the year in restless limbo. Early on in the operation Detective Superintendent John Bassett, the senior investigation officer of the Edzell team, had asked him whether he was being kept informed by his men of their 'entrapment' operation. My father was appalled by the words of the senior officer, implying an illegal procedure. He had been told that Colin Stagg 'was in possession of details' and, with very little information, could only trust the police's judgement and hope for the best.

Meanwhile I remained oblivious and focused instead on enjoying my new life. During the months of May and June 1994, as my first school year was coming to an end, committal proceedings against Colin Stagg were heard in London. Here, the lawyers from the CPS had to prove to the magistrate that the police had a strong enough case for the suspect to face trial. Despite the earlier warning from the CPS that there was insufficient evidence, for reasons that remain unknown they decided to continue with the case and a trial date was set for September.

On 14 September 1994, the trial had barely begun when Mr Justice Ognall ruled all evidence collected through the undercover operation as inadmissible. He referred to the sexually explicit tape-recording voiced by the undercover officer as 'thoroughly reprehensible' and called the behaviour of the police in their pursuit of Colin Stagg 'a substantial attempt to incriminate a suspect by positive and deceptive conduct of the grossest kind'.

Once the judge had ruled that the undercover material would not go before a jury, the CPS decided to offer no further evidence. Colin Stagg was formally acquitted and walked free from court into the spotlight of a national media frenzy.

The fatal errors committed by the police throughout the undercover operation and the flawed decision of the CPS to take the case to trial left the crime unsolved – and the perpetrator at large. Due to the Double Jeopardy rule, a principle central to UK criminal law, Colin Stagg could never be tried again for the same crime, not even if new and indisputable evidence were to be uncovered.

When my father heard the news over the phone, he felt sick to the pit of his stomach. But somehow he managed to keep himself together and to pick me up from school that lunchtime. It would be several days, however, before he found the right moment to explain to me that the man who it was believed had killed my mother was once again on the loose.

Soon after the collapse of the trial, the Commissioner of the Metropolitan Police Service, Sir Paul Condon, informed reporters, 'We are not looking for anyone else,' in connection with the murder. My father was left believing not only that Colin Stagg had got away with murder, but that he was now at large and free to kill again. As long as that remained the case, my father would be forever looking over his shoulder, fearing for my safety.

In the weeks that followed, my father struggled with disturbing thoughts. He was troubled by the recent conversation with my teacher and couldn't bear the idea of handing me over to another psychologist. But when he finally found a quiet moment to sit down and look at my drawings, whatever concerns he had were quickly dispelled. Others might doubt my psychological well-being, but he could clearly see my present passions being reflected. I had been drawing the 'Mysterons' – the baddies in the *Captain Scarlet* cartoons I was watching at home. In the series the other baddie was Captain Black, so if I was going to be drawing him it was no surprise that I would be using a lot of black.

Books, cartoons and stories of all sorts had always been fascinating to me. They inspired and enraptured me, and would lead to extraordinary passions. Whenever I found myself captivated by a character I would immerse myself completely until, in my mind, I became the character. In France, as always, I had an abundance of energy and awoke very early every morning. Most days I would watch TV before breakfast, and it was then that I was exposed to a world of cartoons I had never seen back in England. Most of them were of pretty poor quality, but I watched them just as enthusiastically. My favourite by far was an animated Japanese version of *The Adventures of Tom Sawyer*.

My father, who could barely remember the storyline from his childhood, was surprised to discover how gripping and undated the stories were. I was completely hooked; I started wearing cut-down dungarees and a floppy hat in imitation of Tom, and could often be seen with a stalk of grass hanging from the corner of my mouth to add to the effect. If we went out early, I would insist that my father record the programmes. I laughed at the funny parts and was fascinated by the mischief Tom and his friends got up to.

For weeks I followed the story, until eventually we reached the part where Indian Joe appeared. I picked up right away that Joe was the baddy and before long we got to the scene where one dark night, from behind a bush in a graveyard, Tom watched as Indian Joe attacked his partner in an argument over hidden treasure and stabbed him to death with a knife.

My father, who always kept an eye on what I watched, hovered on the edge of a chair with the remote control in his hand, one eye on the screen, the other on my face. For any child this was potentially the stuff of nightmares. Now that my own nightmares had subsided, would this trigger their return? For any child a scene like that might have been terrifying, but for me it was only a pale shadow of what I had already experienced. Even so, it was a real effort for my father to prevent himself from turning the television off, leaping up and throwing his arms around me. But he knew he couldn't protect me from every potentially frightening moment that came along and restrained himself from saying anything more than, 'Something scary is going to happen …'

It was clear from my rapt expression, however, that I still wanted to watch. My eyes widened as the scene continued to unfold but I showed no sign of wanting to hide my face. When the murder scene had passed, I looked at my father and shivered, as if to say, 'That was scary,' and immediately immersed myself in the cartoon once again.

Watching me, my father decided not to say anything about the scene and wondered what questions were going to come up in the next few days. I had none. He listened out especially carefully over the nights that followed, and my sleep remained calm. Over the following weeks I continued to watch avidly as the story centred upon this violent death. I was more interested in the character of Joe the Indian than any of the others, but whatever thoughts I had about him I kept to myself.

My father was greatly relieved to see how unaffected I seemed. For him, it meant that he would no longer need to scrutinise everything I might come into contact with as he had until then. In a strange way, because of what I'd been through, I was now immune to things that might have once frightened me.

Of all the books I remember reading as a small child, there are a handful that really stand out in my mind. One of these, given to me by my parents when I was very small, was called *Cops and Robbers*. In the story the good, hard-working police officers work day and night to catch the bad, nasty robbers who steal toys from little children and food from the plates of helpless babies.

The book was one of my favourites, a classic tale of the triumph of good over evil. Nonetheless, it always struck me as significant, even at an early age, that the plot gave no explanation as to why the robbers had become robbers in the first place. As I grew older, and in the shadow of my mother's attack, this would become a subject of continuing interest. It was a theme explored in close detail in the *Batman* cartoons I also liked to watch. The plot consisted largely of Batman, the defender of good, reaching out to help those unable to protect themselves from evil. Although Batman's beginning was undoubtedly more tragic than mine, I was probably drawn to the story due to the similarities between his life and my own. At an early age he had witnessed the killing of his parents by a mugger who had attempted to steal their jewellery, and in the aftermath of his parents' death Batman was also to be brought up in an isolated environment by a male figure: his parents' butler.

The thing that fascinated me most, however, was the fact that the so-called 'baddies' had once been nice, innocent 'goodies' who, as a result of an unmerited, scarring experience inflicted upon them, would become the 'baddies' in turn, repeating the same cycle of inflicting evil on someone else. But Batman, the victim of an equally unjust experience, had chosen another path. He had found a way to turn the negative into a positive and the evil into good. And so, as my interest in Batman grew, it was only natural for me to begin going everywhere with a cape, a cardboard mask and an emblem on my chest.

Despite the collapse of the trial, our lives continued as before, apart, perhaps, from my father's increased vigilance whenever there were strangers about.

In the autumn of that year, as the leaves changed colour and began to fall from the trees, Molly went missing. It wasn't the first time she had escaped, but each time my father still worried that she wouldn't come back, and cursed her because he would have to explain to me that my dog was gone.

Eventually, though, Molly would always return, collapsing straight into her bed, exhausted and skinny, but appearing deliriously happy. After a deep sleep, she would once again be her usual self. But this time she had been gone for days and my father was beginning to think that she might be gone for good.

Then one evening she showed up on the front step, whining to be let in. As soon as my father opened the front door, she dragged herself inside and collapsed straight into her bed. This time, however, when we made our way down to breakfast the following morning, Molly was still asleep. She was skinnier than ever and her pads were worn and bleeding. She looked weak and frail, and when she finally awoke she showed no interest in her food.

When my father collected me after school that afternoon, we drove her down to the local animal clinic to have her examined. The vet explained to us that Molly had picked up some sort of bacterial infection from a tick. The illness, he said, killed three out of every four dogs and he offered little chance for her survival.

Hoping for the best, we placed Molly inside a cage at the clinic, with a drip in her leg, and after saying our goodbyes to her, my father and I returned to the house for dinner. Once again, it was just the two of us.

Over the following days, my father dropped me off at school every morning before making his way to the clinic where he spent the following hours squirting food into Molly's mouth with a syringe – although, despite his efforts, most of the liquid dropped straight onto the floor. When lunchtime arrived he would collect me from school and drive us both back to the clinic. We would go through to the back room, which was lined with cages inhabited by all kinds of birds, dogs, cats, rabbits and other animals. All the while Molly lay in her cage looking tired and uninterested, and when I stroked her she didn't respond. Her journey, it seemed, had reached the end.

But a few drops of the liquid my father was feeding her had trickled down her throat after all, and his tender care began to pay off. Within a few days Molly was standing up again and the vet told us that we could take her home. Over the following weeks she lay quietly on her bed and my father continued to force soup down her throat and give her injections morning and evening. In the meantime I went happily about my usual routine, stopping to give her the odd stroke from to time, somehow certain that she was going to be fine.

Even though she still looked painfully thin, with all her bones standing out, my father was finally convinced that she would recover completely when she attempted to bite him one day after one injection too many. By the time Christmas arrived she was almost her old self and once again it was the three of us.

Settled in a solid routine and with a new group of friends, the rest of the year passed uneventfully. I started taking piano lessons once a week and attending judo classes with my neighbour Remy, who lived above the tractors, and my father started playing tennis again in a small municipal club nearby. In the summer I joined in with the group lessons led by the parents of a boy a few years older than me who was already the best player of his age in the country and would go on to be ranked in the world's top ten.

As autumn became winter my father began to write down the children's stories that he had been working on since our break together on the French coast. Drawing inspiration from Molly and me, and all the adventures we shared together in our new home, he created the character of Little Louis, a young explorer who together with his faithful dog embarks on an exciting journey across the globe in search of adventures, hidden treasures and ancient knowledge. After he had read the stories out to me, I would give him my opinion and any suggestions I might have, and once they had finally met my approval we would sketch out the illustrations together on the floor.

Our trips to the UK also become more frequent and we returned for short visits every few months to stay with family and friends. During one of these visits my mother's parents came to collect me in London, and I went off on my own with them to spend the afternoon at their house in Bedfordshire. Whenever I visited their home they would always talk about my mother and encourage me to look through her possessions, carefully stored in her old room. I particularly liked a small wooden box that played a haunting melody when I lifted its lid and an old snow globe from when she was little.

I have a clear memory of my grandfather teaching me to sit at the table with my back to the wall. He explained to me that, this way, I'd always be prepared if I saw a potential threat coming towards me. After giving his words some thought, I decided that this was good advice and that from then on the seat with my back to the wall would always be my preferred place at mealtimes.

Later that afternoon my grandmother drove me back to London and dropped me off at my friend Isaac's house. My father opened the front door to greet us, only to find that my hair had been cut. Sending me into the house to play with Isaac and shutting the door behind him, he walked out to speak to my grandmother in private. Inside he was fuming. He warned my grandmother never to do any such thing again. My well-being, he reminded her, was his responsibility, and it was not their place to make decisions like these without consulting him first. If they chose to do so again, they might not see me in the future.

* * *

In the spring of 1995 one of the hunting dogs that played with Molly in the yard gave birth to a litter of adorable black puppies inside the chicken runs. The father was a Labrador that belonged to the owners of the property and they all looked like tiny versions of Molly. I was intrigued by them, so one afternoon my father and I decided to take a closer look, bringing my friend Remy along with us.

As we entered the chicken runs, we left the heavy metal gate open and stepped inside to play with the newborn puppies. After picking them up and stroking their soft furry bellies to my heart's content, I stepped back to lean against the gate. Moments later, my friend Remy stood up and began to make his way through to the yard outside. But just as he passed me by, he slammed the gate suddenly, squashing my thumb between the hinges. As I lifted my hand, blood was pouring everywhere and my thumb was almost severed.

'I'm going to die! I'm going to die!' I screamed.

Rushing to my side, my father jammed my thumb back into place and we ran as fast as we could to the owner's house next door, squeezing it together all the while.

She was a doctor, so if anyone could help it was her. Her teenage daughter answered and, heading quickly into the kitchen to fetch a bag of ice, she told us that her mother wasn't home but that she'd be arriving very shortly.

Fortunately, her mother was back within minutes and after a quick glance at my hand she bundled us into her car, climbed into the driving seat and we pulled away immediately. The nearest hospital was a half-hour drive away and as I sat in the seat, with my throbbing hand inside a plastic bag, the journey seemed like an eternity.

As soon as we reached the hospital the doctors came running out and rushed me straight into the operating room. I was immediately given an anaesthetic, but they had to act fast and it hadn't yet taken effect when they plunged the needle through the flesh and began stitching my thumb back together. The pain was excruciating. To keep me from writhing in discomfort, they told my father to climb on top of me and hold me down.

Stitch after stitch, I screamed at the top of my lungs as he held onto me, and the doctors worked their way round my thumb. In the end it took over thirty stitches for them to finish the job.

As they bandaged my thumb, the anaesthetic finally began to take effect and at last I started to calm down. I was soon smiling again when the nurse offered to buy me a chocolate bar if I went with her to the machine at the end of the hall.

As my father stood watching, the doctors explained to him that I had every chance of making a full recovery. But the adrenaline inside him was still pumping and he struggled to regain his composure. For him it had been the worst day since we'd left England. The thought that I might lose my thumb had been too much for him to bear. All he could do was hope the experience wouldn't set me back emotionally after the progress that I'd made over the last two and a half years.

On my return to school a few days later, my teachers told me not to worry about the fact that I couldn't write. But so determined was I to continue learning and moving forward that I began writing with my left hand instead. When my thumbnail fell off I returned to the hospital every week to have the flesh burned down so that the new one could grow unobstructed.

The treatment was excruciating, but it was so important for me to continue improving at school that I felt the discomfort much less; or maybe I just thought that if I complained my father would force me to stay at home. Perhaps life was teaching me an early lesson in playing the cards we're dealt. It seems that in life, when one door closes, another opens.

Over the next few months the bones and ligaments grew back and, save for being a little crooked, thanks to the doctors who had operated so efficiently my thumb eventually healed and was almost perfect once again.

After the incident in which my teacher suggested I see a psychiatrist because of my black drawings, the subject had never been mentioned again. Perhaps she was startled by my father's reply – or perhaps it was the fact that, even in a small village far from England, word was beginning to spread that there was a dark secret in our family's past and she chose to leave well alone.

As Christmas 1995 approached, with good grades and able to use my right hand once again, everything seemed to be falling into place for my father and me and we were looking forward to a peaceful holiday season.

But out of the blue I was suddenly being labelled 'hyperactive' and scolded every day by my new teacher. Her threats rapidly escalated, until eventually my father was called in for a talk.

In their meeting, my teacher explained to him that I couldn't sit still, that I talked too much and that I was constantly distracting my classmates. She felt bad about having to punish me every day – after all, despite being a foreigner, my grades were within the top three of my class. The regime, she said, was in many regards overly strict and required young children to sit still for hours on end, but unfortunately that was simply the system and there was nothing she could do but enforce the rules passed down to her from above. As a last resort, she wanted to take me to the school psychiatrist so that he could prescribe the same drugs that were already being administered to some of the other children.

I remember waiting nervously for my father in the courtyard while the meeting took place. Although I couldn't understand why, I felt that I was being treated unjustly and accused of something I hadn't done. My father didn't say much to me when he came out, but I had a feeling that I would soon be changing school.

'Can I speak to André Hanscombe please?' a strange voice enquired in English, when my father answered the telephone in our living room a few days later.

The crushing realisation that a reporter was phoning from abroad struck him heavily. Hardly anyone knew our number and we were not listed in the phone book. The police were unaware of our location and whenever my father had passed on a message to them he had purposefully relayed it through my mother's parents. But somehow we had been tracked down. Caught off guard, my father answered in his best French and pretended not to understand a word before rapidly hanging up.

Our illusion of safety had been shattered. He was certain that it could only be a matter of time before someone showed up at the door. And where the press could find us, others could too.

Soon afterwards, on our return home from a shopping trip, we unpacked the bags from the boot of the car and went inside the house for a snack. My father stepped outside again momentarily to throw the rubbish into the bin when an unfamiliar car pulled up at the gate. Two strangers climbed out and began to walk towards him. He froze, his heart hammering in his chest. The strangers had not yet spoken, but my father was under no illusions as to who these people were.

'André?' the first began. 'We just want to –'

'Get out! Go away!' my father shouted. 'You don't know how much harm you cause.' The strength of his outburst caught the strangers off guard. Shamefaced, they mumbled vague apologies before climbing back into their car and driving away.

Just at that very moment I emerged through the front door. They had gone seconds earlier and I had just missed them. My father was stony-faced and as we made our way back into the house he didn't mention a word about the unwelcome intruders.

A few days later an envelope arrived, bearing the postmark of a nearby town. Inside was a scrawled handwritten note. The writing was difficult to read, but the letter said they were sorry for disturbing our privacy and promised to never bother us again or reveal either our location or phone number to anyone. It was unsigned; no name appeared anywhere on the piece of paper or the envelope.

Several weeks later my father's worst suspicions were confirmed. Using his contacts, my maternal grandfather was able to track down the reporters who had sent the letter. Despite their promise, they had already put our details into circulation.

Anyone could find us now.

CHAPTER 12

ON THE RUN AGAIN: NEW LANDS

'The only thing that is constant is change.'

Heraclitus

Our illusion of safety had been shattered, and with our address in free circulation my father realised that we would have to move on once again.

For the time being he decided to keep the true reason for our move a secret, and told me instead that we were moving to learn new languages and to have fun; and that, once again, we were moving to where winters would be warmer.

Although our surroundings had been perfect as a hideaway from all the pressures we had found ourselves under in England, other complications had arisen in our lives. We were too isolated and in such a backwater my father had become a magnet for unwanted female attention, which only served to complicate our life even further. Moreover, now that I had been labelled hyperactive by my teacher it would be impossible for me to remain at the same school without being medicated.

At first, my father was unsure of where we should go. He had thought that we could settle down in a small town somewhere in the Italian countryside and attempt to make a new start once again. But with fond memories from his travels playing tennis and only a short drive away, he finally decided that we should cross the border into Spain instead. Over the following weeks we practised Spanish together every evening to prepare for the move. Following our easy learning cassette course, we would repeat out loud the phrases we heard on the tape:

'*Hola, buenos dias*' – 'Hello, and good day.'

'*Venden pilas?*' – 'Do they sell batteries?'

Even though I would soon be leaving my new friends behind, I was excited about the move and showed no regret whatsoever. 'When we've finished in the new land can we go to another land and learn that language?' I asked my father one day. 'I want to go to all the lands and learn all the languages!'

The Christmas holidays were now just around the corner. And as soon as my break began, we headed towards the border in our old grey Volvo, looking for a new home.

But despite my initial excitement the whole trip turned into something of a nightmare. Arriving at the border after several hours' drive, my father realised that he had left our passports on the kitchen table and we had to drive all the way back home again to collect them. By the time we finally made it across the border the light was fading, we saw nothing but ugly places, the heating broke down in the car and, to cap things off, it began to snow.

Tired, hungry and cold, I began to complain from the back seat. My father was by then beyond exhaustion and could barely see his way in the heavy snow. Constantly on the verge of an accident, we headed miles away from our planned route, to a place where he knew for certain there was a hotel. It was late when we arrived, but we managed to find pizza in a deserted town square before making our way back to our room to spend a warm, snug night.

I awoke early the next morning and, while my father continued to doze, I watched cartoons in Spanish at the foot of the bed. As the day grew lighter, I went to the window to take a look outside. Through the glass I could see a line of children in anoraks, beanies and backpacks, on their way to school. Something about the sounds they made was both fascinating and exotic to me.

With snow thick on the ground, we were forced to head back home, but on our next trip the following week my father brought along a map, marking several points of interest dotted around the outskirts of Barcelona. He wanted us to live near a big city, but not in a big city as he believed 'City life is no good for children – and no good for dogs.'

Our first stop was alongside some tennis courts surrounded by palm trees, and overlooked by forest-covered mountains, with their dramatic skyline beyond. But it was lunchtime when we arrived and everything was already closed down, so we drove on to the next village, where an estate agent showed us a house with a swimming pool so green and overgrown that it could easily have been home to a legion of leeches and snakes. We moved on to look at yet more places, and by the end of the day we'd come full circle and were back at the first village once again.

As we sat in the car my father explained to me that there were no estate agents to be found. It had been a long day and it was getting dark, so he wanted to get back to our hotel to rest. But from the back seat I told him to 'Try in there' as I pointed to a building across the street.

'That isn't an estate agent's, Alex – it's an architect's office. Those are plans in the window, not pictures of houses to rent.'

But I insisted. I had been on my best behaviour all day and was certain of what I'd seen. In the end, my father decided to humour me. We climbed out of the car and headed over to the office, where in his best pidgin Spanish he attempted to ask the receptionist if they had any houses to rent. 'Yes,' she replied, to his surprise, asking us to come back the next day.

We returned the next morning and the estate agent and his secretary showed us three beautiful houses with colourful gardens, a large swimming pool and an old, stone pond populated by oriental ducks, each of them sharing spectacular views of the nearby mountain. They were undeniably impressive, but already furnished and only really suitable for holiday guests. What we needed was a home for the two of us, Molly and all our furniture.

'I'm going to show you another one, but I don't think you'll like it,' the estate agent told us, in a discouraging manner.

Driving back across the village, we parked on a quiet street next to a large plantation of palm trees. As I stepped out of the car I looked up at the house which stood on the corner. It looked abandoned. The shutters were stuck open, the front door was rotting, and the letterbox was jammed with old circulars and misdirected post.

Pushing the post aside, the estate agent forced the door open and began to lead us into the house. It was dark, the lights weren't working, and as we climbed the stairs there were drops of cement and paint splattered across the floor tiles. But as soon as the shutters were rolled up and the windows opened, the house was immediately filled with light. The building may have been dirty and neglected, but the view of the mountains was nothing less than spectacular.

Over the next few days we saw more villages and more houses, but this was the one my father had set his heart on, even though it was further from the city than he had originally intended. After bargaining the price down and discounting the first month's rent in exchange for the work that needed to be done, we made our way back to the border, tired but deeply satisfied.

When I returned to school after my Christmas break, my father rented a van and filled it with our belongings. While I was in class, he headed back across the border without letting anyone know where he was going. When the neighbours asked if we were moving, my father told them that we'd be storing our furniture with my mother's parents, who had recently bought a holiday home in a nearby village, and that we were going to live in America for a year.

My father felt bad about telling them a lie, but the press was on our tail and where the press could find me so could others. As far as he knew, the killer was once again on the loose and the police had warned him to be cautious.

Before informing my teacher that we would soon be leaving, and in order to make sure our stories were consistent, my father explained to me that he was telling everyone that we would be going to live in America for a year. I could still remember all too well the press waiting on our doorstep in London and, without letting me know that they were now close by, we both agreed that we should make it as hard as possible for them to find us if they ever happened to turn up in France after we'd left.

In the week leading up to our move, I posted a goodbye letter to Laure via one of my father's friends in Arizona so that the postmark on the envelope would corroborate our story.

A few days later, my father pulled up in the yard one evening after a final trip to Spain. It was time to say goodbye to my friends Remy and Audrey. They were both sad to see me leave: we had shared endless adventures together running free through the fields and I'd miss them greatly. Closing the front door behind us my father and I went back into the house to spend the last night in what had been our secret hideaway for the past three years. It was the beginning of February 1996.

The following morning, before the break of dawn, we packed the Volvo with the last of our belongings and, with Molly in the back seat, we headed towards the border. This time we weren't going back.

Our new village lay across a wide valley, surrounded by mountains and thick woodlands that exuded pure, clean air every night. In contrast with our home in France, we now found ourselves within walking distance of almost everything we needed. My father would no longer have to drive me back and forth every day to school, or to any of my other activities, and when I was old enough I'd be able to walk everywhere on my own. We were also less than an hour's drive from Barcelona, near the coast and within easy reach of the Pyrenees.

The garage occupied the entire ground floor, and on the first floor there was a kitchen, a small bathroom and a large open living room that extended out onto a narrow balcony with a panoramic view of the mountains. My father took the biggest room on the top floor for himself and told me to choose from the other three. I chose the second largest, with a balcony door that opened out over the same spectacular view as the living room below. I was ecstatically happy, even though I fell down the stairs the very first day and knocked out one of my front teeth.

As we were approaching the Easter holidays, I wouldn't be able to attend the local school until the new term began, so in the meantime I joined the local judo club, where on the very first day I made friends with Jordi and Iker, two boys who were to be in my class.

Before my first day at school, my father sat me down and explained that we should keep our personal circumstances to ourselves. In France we had never broadcast the fact that my mother had been killed, but slowly the word had spread across the village. Our family background, he said, was nobody else's business. Being open before had only caused unnecessary problems for us. If anyone were to ask me about my mother, I could simply tell them that she had died when I was little. If they were still curious I could tell them that she had died in an accident, and if they insisted further I could say it was a car accident.

In the end I only ever used the story of my mother dying in a car accident on a couple of occasions before I realised that it didn't feel right. It wasn't genuine, so I decided instead that I would give away nothing more than the fact that my mother had died in an accident. Most people who asked were well intentioned, but if they chose to pursue the issue I preferred to tell them it was a private matter which was none of their business, rather than telling an outright lie. Two wrongs don't make a right was a phrase my father often used, and this was certainly a case in point.

Settling in to school was in many ways easier than it had been in France. The regime was much more relaxed and no one ever suggested I was hyperactive again. For the first few months my teacher gave me extra attention, speaking to me in French every day until I was able to learn both the local languages, Catalan and Spanish, in little over three months.

Just as in France, the children in my class thought that having a foreigner amongst them was very exotic, something that was especially true of the girls. And, with Jordi and Iker from judo by my side, I found the transition to our new life as smooth as it could possibly be. We were soon inseparable, spending as much of our time together as we could, rotating whose home we went to for lunch and sleeping over at each other's houses at the weekends.

While Jordi lived on a street nearby, Iker lived in an old farmhouse out in the countryside with his younger brother and soon-to-come sister. His family had dogs, cats, chickens and goats. During the months and years to come we would find ourselves involved in a long list of adventures as we ran free over the mountainside with the seasons changing around us. In the summer we peered under tree trunks looking for snakes, which we steered into glass bottles, punching holes in the lids for them to breathe. We would then take them to school to show off proudly to our friends and, when we were finally done and had lost interest in them altogether, cautious to avoid a poisonous bite, carefully unscrew the lids and toss the bottles gently to the ground, waiting until the snakes slithered off into the wild again.

Our teacher would soon remark upon the fact that we were all born in the Chinese year of the snake. The three of us were full of mischief, and whenever the opportunity presented itself, always quick to stack the odds in our favour. On one occasion we decided to wind the clock on the classroom wall forward in order to finish early every day. Just as a python wraps itself around its victim, tightening up ever so slightly with every exhalation, over the course of several weeks, whenever our teacher left the room to run an errand, we added a few extra seconds to the clock.

It didn't take long for us to reap the fruits of our labour. Not only were we the first to be let out into the playground during our break and the first to finish at the end of every day, but we also gained five minutes of downtime between every class while we waited for the teachers to change rooms. But, as is often the case with greed, in the end we went too far. Heady with success, we ended up over-winding the clock and our teacher suddenly realised it was proving strangely unreliable. Eventually it dawned on her that perhaps human intervention and not electronic malfunction might be the cause of its poor timekeeping. She probably suspected us, but we were never caught.

My father was delighted to see how quickly I had settled in, and how tight my new friends and I were becoming. He'd been on his own since my mother passed away, but during that first year in Spain he met his first girlfriend. I liked her. She played basketball for the local team and whenever she came over to the house we would bounce the ball back and forth between us, shooting at a small hoop on the garage wall. Their relationship couldn't have lasted for more than a year, but in the end they remained good friends.

Just as in France, our excursions into the fields continued. Every morning before class my father and I rose before sunrise and set off on bike rides and runs together with Molly, who always had the time of her life exploring new scents and chasing rabbits through the bushes.

At weekends, Jordi, Iker and I began travelling to judo competitions. In his youth our teacher qualified for the Olympics – and even though he wasn't able to participate due to a back injury, he was extremely passionate about the art and we all respected him greatly. He dedicated himself wholeheartedly to accompanying us to competitions and training camps up and down the country, as well as to different parts of Europe.

Our teacher was also Iker's uncle and his passion for judo was followed closely by his love for motocross bikes. He stored his impressive collection at the house of Iker's grandparents, who also lived out in the countryside. During those first summers in Spain we visited their house regularly to swim in their pool, but what always fascinated us most were all the motorbikes parked in the garage, at the other end of the yard. As we were still so young we weren't allowed to take them out, so we just climbed on them instead, making believe.

One day, however, an exception was made and Iker was allowed to ride a small quad bike on his own, without supervision. After I'd watched him circle the grounds around me for ages, he finally let me have a go myself. But as soon as I pulled out onto the narrow track I steered slightly too far to the side, driving off a small precipice and landing in the middle of a thorny blackberry bush below.

Needless to say, both my friend and his uncle milked that story to the very last drop!

It seems there are certain stories one can never forget, perhaps due to the lesson they present. One day I was horsing around in my room with Jordi when he accidentally knocked my alarm clock off the desk, and it smashed to the floor. Although I was initially upset, I quickly saw an opportunity to make things work in my favour. I told Jordi that the alarm clock was in fact my father's and that if he found out it was broken he'd be furious. Seeing how worried he was, and knowing what a noble nature he had, I told him that, if he just paid me the price of the alarm clock out of his pocket money, it would all be OK and I wouldn't have to tell my father.

He duly paid up, but as is always the case with dark secrets, sooner or later they inevitably come to the surface. Jordi had a close relationship with his mother and eventually he told her about what had happened. She confronted my father, who then confronted me, and I was forced to write a letter of apology and return the money.

I certainly felt bad: humiliated for being caught, and guilty for tricking one of my best friends. But I soon felt much better once the issue had finally been resolved.

The summer of 1997 was long and hot. The fifth anniversary of my mother's murder came and went, as it had always done, unnoticed by me. From the very beginning, my father had decided not to make an issue of occasions like these because the two of them always believed that every day of the year was an opportunity for celebration or fond remembrance.

Shortly before my eighth birthday I went to stay with my grandparents for a week. It was the middle of the summer holidays and I hadn't seen them since the previous Christmas so, as always, I was looking forward to seeing them again. Before our move to Spain they had bought a small holiday house in a peaceful French village, near to where we used to live.

My uncle Mark, who was on holiday with his partner, came to collect me and the three of us drove up from the village together. I had always got along well with my uncle. He first looked after me when I was only months old and my parents went out to see Anita Baker in concert one evening. In later years he had bought me a small Swiss army knife and taken me mushroom hunting. Although I detested their taste, during our time in France I had become very keen to find them and knew all about the local varieties.

A few days after our arrival my uncle and his partner returned home, and as my grandfather wouldn't be arriving until later in the week, in the meantime it was just me and my grandmother, who was busy overseeing the workmen who were building an extension to the house.

We spent the first days taking it easy in the garden, swimming in the pool and preparing the food I liked best, until one afternoon my grandmother suggested a haircut. My hair was loose and curly as I normally wore it, but I was perfectly happy with the idea, and even told her how I wanted to have it cut. She told me there was no need to tell my father, and that we could just let him know later on. Unlike the first haircut where she had taken me to a professional, this time my grandmother went to work herself with some nail scissors, chopping off my fringe at the hairline, and leaving the rest almost as long as it was before. Needless to say, the result wasn't exactly what I had anticipated.

The next day my grandmother took me to visit Isaac, my best friend from England, whose family had recently moved to France and were living in a village nearby. She left me in their care and I slept over that night. The next morning my friend's family noticed me going from room to room, checking on my reflection, attempting to pull on whatever was left of my fringe in order to make it look longer than it actually was. Although they said nothing at the time, they would later comment that my grandmother's haircut had left me looking like the 'village idiot'.

When my father arrived to collect me at the end of the week I was still swimming in the pool, but as soon as he lifted me out of the water I clung to him with all my strength. I stared into his eyes and wouldn't say a word.

'What has she done to him?' my father snapped at my grandfather.

'He's had a wonderful holiday and you're now upsetting him!' he fired back immediately.

A heated discussion ensued, until moments later my grandmother stepped out of the house exclaiming, 'He said he wanted to have a haircut,' before disappearing back into the house again.

I remember being consumed by a feeling of guilt I had never experienced before, but at the time I couldn't understand why. Only as the years went by was I able to see through the complexity of the situation. My grandmother, who had already been warned by my father never to cut my hair again, had chosen to do so regardless. By persuading me to say the words 'I want my hair cut', I had unknowingly become her accomplice. Not only did she use this in her defence, but it put me on the spot to see if I would defend her, because I had in all truth voiced those words.

The guilt I felt inside had been part of a subconscious plan – one in which my well-being was placed at stake to break my father's boundaries and see how much he was prepared to tolerate. Just like a gambler, all the chips had been placed on this one big bet.

As soon as I finished changing into dry clothes my father picked up my bag, threw our stuff into the car and we drove off without saying goodbye.

The next day was my eighth birthday, and the only thing I had asked for was a trip on a pedalo out into the bay. Yet as we arrived at the beach that morning I was crying, and as soon as we got out of the car I clung to my father. No matter how much he attempted to reassure me, I wouldn't let go and eventually we gave up on the ride altogether and decided to drive back home.

That evening my father phoned my grandparents to inform them of the consequences of their actions. If only for my sake, he wanted to salvage the situation. My grandfather answered the phone and one by one my father began to read the points he had noted on a sheet of paper. He reminded him that he had never given permission for a haircut and that there had already been a precedent. The haircut – which was humiliating in itself – wasn't the issue but that, as the parent, he should be consulted first over any decisions concerning my well-being.

There were other issues arising from the visit. Perhaps to protect me from the influence of my uncle and his partner, my grandmother had taken me out of my room to sleep in her bed, even though she was aware of the fact that after my mother's murder it had taken my father several years for me to sleep on my own the whole night through.

Before the trip my father had carefully prepared my clothing and toys because he wanted me to have my own things when I travelled so as to maintain my sense of comfort and security. But my grandmother had bought new clothes and toys instead, and my bag was kept aside. Memories, which remain with me to this day, caused me to feel deeply upset.

As the call came to an end my father reminded my grand-father of the fact that they were grandparents for the first time, and of a child who had been through an extremely traumatic situation. Given my grandmother's recent actions my father said that he would never leave me alone with her again.

'What do you want us to do?' my grandfather asked.

'I always try to apologise to Alex when I make mistakes,' my father replied.

'OK,' my grandfather answered, agreeing to call back the next day.

After the upset of the last few days, my father didn't want to wait around the house with me feeling miserable, so the next morning we made a trip to a theme park with some friends, and from almost the moment we arrived I started to lighten up again.

When my grandfather phoned the following evening, I was sitting on my father's knee. He wanted me to hear their apology for myself.

'We're not going to apologise,' my grandfather began. 'You've upset him! He's had a wonderful holiday and we're perfect grandparents. Alex's grandmother is my wife and the woman I will be living with for the rest of my life. We obviously don't get on, so we'll see Alex again when he's 16. You'll send us photos and videos in the meantime.'

Over the following months my father continued to ask me from time to time whether I wished to see them, but I always said no.

Later in the year we received a written apology, and my father explained to me that my grandparents had said sorry. I remained silent. He asked me once again if I wished to see them, but as always I said no.

When Christmas arrived, my great-grandmother phoned us from the nursing home where she now lived. In her eighties, it was the first time she had ever dialled our number of her own accord. I had last seen her the previous Christmas, at my grandparents' home in France, and even though she was a very elderly lady we had always got on really well, spending long hours together playing cards. Ironically one of the games we used to play was called 'Happy Families' and my great-grandmother often remarked how good I was, as I often ended up winning the game.

But just as my father was about to hand over the phone to me, my great-grandmother suddenly exclaimed, 'I think it's wicked of you not to allow his grandparents to see him!' My father was shocked to find out that an elderly lady, who had already suffered the loss of her only granddaughter, had been left to believe that my grandparents had been banned from seeing their only grandchild. 'The only thing I'm going to say is that there are two sides to every story,' my father replied. 'Feel free to phone any time you like,' he added.

I chatted happily with her for a few minutes, before going off about my day. As it was Christmas, I had plenty of new toys to play with and the conversation was of little significance for me at the time. Several months later I spoke to her for the last time before she passed away.

CHAPTER 13

THE REPORTER

'Most of the time, with time, tragedy
becomes comedy.'

Smokey Robinson

Almost nine years had passed since my mother's murder, and with the case still unsolved the press interest in me and my father had not diminished. It was early spring in 2001 when I arrived home from school one lunchtime and my father told me that the press had tracked us down. He had been playing tennis at the local courts when the postman tipped him off that a 'foreigner' was lurking in the neighbourhood, asking questions about us. Steaming mad, my father knew there was only one explanation. Driving back to the house as fast as he could, he parked the car in the garage and made his way quickly up the stairs. As he opened the balcony door on the top floor, he spotted a car parked at the end of the road with a man sitting inside, staring towards our house.

His blood was boiling. Only days before our departure from France another reporter had intruded onto our property, and my father had warned him that if he didn't leave right away he would be forced to come out with his shotgun. Now, as he found himself in yet another confrontation in our new home, he began walking directly towards the car while the stranger inside pretended to be busy, looking the other way. My father knocked on the window, and as the man attempted to open the door he told him, in no uncertain terms, to leave. 'But André, I just want to talk to you,' the stranger replied, as if to insinuate that his feelings had been hurt. Their strategy was always to address us by our first names, as if they were long-lost friends, even though they never revealed their own, and their actions showed no sign of genuine friendliness whatsoever. What they really wanted was to invade our privacy so that they could sell the story. For them, it was a simple trade: our lives, in return for their livelihoods.

'If he ever comes back again, I'll slash his tyres!' I exclaimed passionately when my father finished explaining what had happened. I was happy in Spain and didn't want to have to pack up and leave my friends behind all over again.

For days my father was consumed by doubts. 'Should we move again as we had done before? Where would we go? Would we find a place better than this? And if so, what would be the cost emotionally?'

He knew that this was a crucial stage of my life and wanted to make the right decision. After turning the subject over thoroughly in his mind he concluded that any difficulty involved in staying behind wouldn't outweigh the positives. He wasn't going to allow us to be driven from our home a third time. This time we would stay put.

The weeks and months that followed were quiet until, one night when I left by coach for a week-long skiing trip with my school, my father received a phone call. The man on the line claimed to be a member of the national police force. Not long before there had been a series of fatal bus crashes involving groups of schoolchildren and the image immediately flashed through my father's mind. But in spite of his initial fears, from the random questions he was asked it soon dawned on him that this was nothing more than another attempt by the press to get a story, no matter what the cost.

Not long after, our bank manager telephoned to inform us that a British reporter had called their offices, attempting to extract information concerning our whereabouts. Until then our bank manager had never found himself in a situation like this: he was appalled by the behaviour of the press and extremely concerned about our privacy.

Over the years to come, in an attempt to stop the insidious press intrusion into our lives, my father would give his consent to several newspaper interviews. Caught between a rock and a hard place, he hoped that the occasional, controlled update at strategic moments might stop much of the intrusion. But in the end this never worked out as planned and the press continued to pursue us and to run stories on us, most of them a long way from the truth.

By the end of our first year in Spain, my father had begun to search for an au pair. From the moment we left England he had been looking after me on his own and had come to the decision that he wanted someone who could at the very least supervise me at lunchtimes and after school while he was busily involved in tennis once again. He thought too that I might benefit from having a female presence in the house. But things didn't quite go to plan and by the time I was 12 we'd had seven different girls living in our house.

Our first au pair was French. Christelle was 25 and arrived the Easter before my eighth birthday. Her mother was from Tahiti but her father, who was a sailor, had taken her back to France with him as a baby, handing her over to his parents to look after. On the first night of her stay I crept into her room to place a lifelike rubber snake under the sheet of her bed. Some time later I heard her scream as I lay in my own bed, chuckling with satisfaction. By the next morning she'd managed to recover her composure and accepted my practical joke with good humour, but she admitted that she had been terrified, as snakes were the one thing she just couldn't stand.

She soon found herself a boyfriend in the village who loved outdoor sports and, together with his younger brother, they often took me along on cycling and climbing trips.

Even though we didn't always get along, I liked Christelle and we had lots of fun together. She was genuinely fond of me and was the only au pair who would later come back to visit.

Our second au pair was from Sweden. Gentle and confident, Linda had just returned from the US where she had earned herself a basketball scholarship at a junior college, and during her stay with us she joined the local team. In the end she only stayed for three months, because she wanted to live somewhere with warmer winters.

Our third au pair, also Swedish and also called Linda, was almost the exact opposite and in the end she also left early. She didn't mind the winters but was under the impression that we were much nearer to the bright lights.

The fourth au pair was Yvette, a 22-year-old Hungarian. Her previous employers treated her like a slave and she felt the need to be justifying her presence twenty-four hours a day, seven days a week, and was constantly tidying, washing and polishing. The house had never been so clean, but her sudden bursts of anger became too much for my father and, after finding her yelling at me one day, he gave her notice to leave.

By then it occurred to him that an older grandmother figure might add greater stability to our home life so he decided to hire a Cuban lady in her mid-fifties who had given lessons to Fidel Castro's guerrillas as a teenage girl.

Eunice was an ex-headmistress with two grown-up sons who had left her country after her husband passed away, in order to escape the hardships of everyday life. Her intention was now to marry a rich local man who could ensure that she lived out the rest of her days in comfort and security. Given that her physique was far from suited to the slopes and hills around us, her legs ached from the very beginning and she left for days at a time to recover. Eventually, after six months of working on and off, Eunice never returned.

The sixth au pair was a local girl in her late twenties. Ignoring my father's requests to prepare the nutritious snacks he wanted, she decided to buy sweets from the local shop instead. One day I visited her house and, as I looked around, I noticed that some CDs that had disappeared from my room some time ago were now sitting on her shelves. As diplomatically as I could I took them back for myself, but inside I was fuming. In the end she lasted eight months before leaving in turn. Lucie, the seventh au pair, was from the Czech Republic, and was 22 when she arrived. Our rooms were divided by a thin wall, and over time an endless series of petty disputes would arise over the sharing of the telephone line and the use of common spaces.

From the very beginning I did my best to convince my father that we didn't need anyone else in the house, and that I was, at 11, more than capable of looking after myself. In my eyes, I was already cooking my own meals, cleaning up after myself and taking care of the tasks my father had assigned to me. 'Why can't we get rid of her?' became a question I asked him frequently. 'When you live under your own roof you can make your own decisions,' he always replied.

Lucie loved tennis. She had played as a young girl, but her parents didn't have the means with which to support her. Soon, my father came to a new agreement with her: in return for his coaching and financial support she would continue to work in the house. He considered that she had talent and, with the right training, had the potential to go a long way. The news that she would be staying on with us even longer than I could have possibly imagined, however, was a big blow.

By the beginning of my twelfth year I found myself one of the smallest in my class. All my friends were growing up fast and I suddenly felt left behind, which meant that judo, tennis, football, athletics and all the other sports I was taking part in were now much harder. The situation irritated me greatly and I complained to my father, who tried to reassure me that Mediterranean people tend to grow early but also stop growing early. My mother, he said, was 5 feet 9 inches tall, and I was likely to be taller than her at the very least.

Eventually, however, my concerns began to influence my father's thinking and he found himself wondering whether I was getting enough nutrition from my diet. Vegetarianism of any kind, while becoming far more popular, was still looked down upon, especially in countries like France and Spain, and in the days before the internet was readily available to everyone accurate information about the benefits or drawbacks of such a diet was hard to find. The general consensus was that a diet of fish and meat was healthier and, due to a lack of alternative information, conventional thinking was weighing heavily on my father.

My mother had been a vegetarian in the days when it was frowned upon and mocked by many, but she strongly believed the benefits were measurable and had been determined to raise me in the same way. I was in the middle of my twelfth year when my father announced to me that I was now going to eat fish – whether I liked it or not. I had never eaten the flesh of an animal before. Not only had I always detested the sight and smell of meat, but my body had been educated to reject it. I felt that my father was interfering not only with my own wishes but with my mother's as well. I felt so strongly about it that I would have preferred the possible risk of staying the height I was, accepting any disadvantages it might bring, rather than to eat flesh.

At first I attempted as best as I could to swallow the fish, but as soon as I did the gag reflex immediately set in and I would vomit it straight back out onto my plate. The situation led to a great deal of conflict between my father and me, and a very similar situation to that in France years before ended up playing itself out all over again.

At mealtimes I wasn't allowed to leave until the fish on my plate was finished so I began feeding it to Molly under the table instead. But soon my father started to become suspicious of her sudden eagerness to hover around me while I ate, so I resorted to placing the fish inside a napkin hidden in my pocket and throwing it down the toilet later. Paradoxically, my diet was now even less nutritious than before.

Things came to a head on a summer visit to see Isaac and his family in France for my thirteenth birthday.

Lunch was fish that day, and even though it was my birthday my father decided I was going to eat the same as everyone else. When lunch arrived we all sat down at the table together, until eventually everyone finished their desserts and left – while I remained alone at the table with the fish still on my plate. In private, my father explained to Isaac's mother that he was going to have no choice but to give in, as my willpower was so strong that it would most definitely end badly.

But Isaac's mother thought I was behaving like a rude, spoilt child and insisted I shouldn't be allowed at any cost to get away with not eating the fish on my plate. My father told her that, if she wanted to try on her own, she could, but that he had already done his best and wasn't willing to insist any further. Knowing his mere presence in the room was a provocation to me, he went to the furthest end of the house to distract himself.

In the meantime, Isaac's mother did her best to encourage me to eat the fish, but, unsuccessful in her efforts, she was forced to seek my father out. 'He has to eat it,' she insisted.

'I do what I can,' my father replied, 'but if I can't, it's not worth it. I'm a single parent and Alex and I still have to live together afterwards.'

My father respected her views; she was a mother of five with an enormous amount of experience to draw from and he'd always given her advice a great deal of weight. This time, there was no doubt whatsoever in her mind about the appropriate course of action, so my father prepared himself for the battle of wills to follow.

Minutes later he returned to the room, and a violent scene with lots of shouting and screaming ensued. But there was still no way I was going to eat the fish. It wasn't the first time a scene like this had ended violently. A few months before, an argument had ensued and, as tempers flared, I had threatened my father with a large kitchen knife. Frustrated by his ongoing threats to throw me out of the house, while treating the au pair as if she was his own daughter, there's no doubt in my mind that if he hadn't walked away right there and then, the situation would have ended badly.

In the weeks that followed I sat down at the table to face trial by them. The au pair voiced a long list of complaints about me from her notebook, while my father threatened to throw me out on the street again or put me in a foster home. I didn't feel loved by him in the way I thought I deserved. More than once I returned home from school at lunchtime, only to find the lock on the door had been changed.

As we found ourselves facing yet another confrontation, this time in Isaac's dining room, rather than enjoying time with our friends, my father and I vented all our frustrations, and shouted venomously at one another. Minutes later, Isaac's mother returned to the room and asked us to leave their house. Her husband and children had been huddling in the room next door, terrified by the scene unfolding between my father and me. 'All of my children would have done anything I asked of them by now,' she exclaimed.

As if to match the intensity of our moods, a forest fire erupted on the journey home, the motorway was cut off and we were forced to take a twisty coastal road. Some time later, we sat together in silence on a beachfront bench, looking out to sea and contemplating the situation.

Years later, when the heat of those moments had long since cooled, my father would confide to me that he was not only proud of the fact that I was strong enough to stand up for myself, but reassured that I wouldn't give in to his or anyone else's wishes if I felt I was right. He wasn't sure I would have made it any other way. But at the time I had no knowledge of this, and all there seemed to be was the ongoing confrontation between us.

Isaac's mother was a good friend and she had genuinely sought to offer her best advice. But, understandably, she was unable to comprehend fully the dynamics of our relationship from the outside. Until that moment her family had only seen the bright side of our life, and as soon as the dark side was revealed they had found themselves confounded and unable to respond.

That was the last time I saw Isaac. Nothing, however, can take away the connection we shared or the good times we had together. Over the years his family offered support in moments of great need, and to this day I still dream about him from time to time. I have always known that one day, in some way, our paths will cross again.

CHAPTER 14

SEARCH FOR FREEDOM

'Tough times never last, but tough people do.'

Dr Robert Schuller

I can't remember exactly how skateboarding came into my life, but it seems that all my friends not only had mountain bikes, but hidden away somewhere at the back of their garage there was also an old skateboard gathering dust – and even though everyone was used to taking their bike out regularly, no one really knew how to skate.

Because of this, a group of older kids came up with the idea of sitting on their boards as if they were go-carts and racing down the steep, cemented roads that descended through treacherous twists and turns from high above the residential areas. And every now and then a bunch of us younger kids would get together with them and climb for several kilometres before reaching the very top, where a statue of the Sacred Heart stood overlooking the village. Once there, we would all sit expectantly on our skateboards and, as soon as the 'go' signal was given, push off as fast as we could with our hands, gathering more and more speed as we raced all the way back down the hill.

Although we were never on a completely level playing field, as certain boards were much smoother and faster, it was always the person with the most guts who would win because there was really no limit to how fast you could go – if you were willing.

My passion for skateboarding sparked from there and only continued to grow in the years that followed.

It's hard to define what pulls a person towards something so strongly that it soon takes over their life completely. Vedic literature, which originates from ancient India, says that all our current tendencies are being influenced in some shape or form by experiences accumulated during previous existences. What is certain is that a large number of skaters come from broken homes and difficult backgrounds, and skateboarding has been a positive outlet through which to channel that negative energy into something constructive.

I soon became close friends with two neighbouring kids, who shared the same passion, and we began to spend almost every moment of our free time skating together. As they were both several years older than me – 16 to my 13 – they nicknamed me 'El Xic', which translates roughly as 'The Little One'. From the very beginning they took their role of overseeing me to heart and always kept a close eye out for me.

The elder of the two was a big punk and hardcore music fan who during our time together introduced me to all his favourite bands, encouraging me always to think for myself and live life on my own terms.

The village had no skateboarding culture whatsoever so we were forced to become as creative as possible with what little was available, and as much of the surrounding area was sloped, and not ideal for us, we spent most of our time in a public car park and a couple of nearby village squares. When the summer holidays arrived we had more time on our hands and began to build our own ramps and boxes in our garages and take them out onto the street.

My non-skateboarding friends used to call me a masochist because of all the injuries I suffered from falls: dented shins, broken bones, gashes that had to be stitched up, and even knocking myself unconscious. But it was always clear to me that you couldn't develop new skills or continue to push the edge of your own envelope without coming up against failures. If you never fell, then you weren't getting any better.

Over the years that followed, a number of long-running disputes would arise between nearby neighbours, the local police and ourselves, fuelled to a great extent by their dislike of skateboarding, and their ongoing attempts to stop us. Conflictive situations became part of everyday life; whenever we were skating in public squares one of the neighbours would eventually come down to complain and a heated argument would ensue, often ending in a fight, so that sooner or later the police would show up on the scene to give us a warning and send us home. We found ourselves caught between a rock and a hard place; the town hall wouldn't provide a space for us, but neither could we skate in public places.

The fact that the background of the officers who came after

us wasn't exactly clean only served to increase the tension between us. One of them was a small-time ex-coke dealer, and the other used to race illegally on public roads. In an attempt to beat his own record he had crashed and rolled several cars over the years. My father and I had even helped him pick up a second-hand hot hatch with our trailer some years before.

In order to escape the ongoing confrontations my friends and I began commuting to the nearest city a couple of times a week, where we could make use of a skatepark and some good spots on the street. Travelling by train was always an adventure, and it became the norm for us to sneak on without paying in order to have money to spare when we arrived at the other end. If the ticket inspector came too close for comfort we would just slip into another wagon at the next stop. Our system worked flawlessly most of the time, but as a back-up plan we memorised a false address and phone number for the occasions when we were caught and fined.

Whenever we were in the city we dropped by the local skate shop to admire all the gear. But it wasn't the cheapest of hobbies, and no matter how much we saved on train fares we were never able to afford the stuff we wanted. Instead, duct tape was the temporary solution I always carried around in my rucksack to fix the rips in my shoes and stick the ends of my board together when they started to come apart from wear.

Eventually we became friends with the local skaters, who had a great appreciation for hip-hop culture and graffiti art. They spent most of their time skating in the same square, but every now and then they'd invite us for a tour of the city's best spots. It was only a matter of time, however, before people living nearby reported us to the police and officers showed up on the scene, asking for our names, addresses and checking all our records.

But for us the positives always outweighed the negatives. It was inspiring to watch people skating at a high level and we always returned recharged. We skated every day without fail, attempting to emulate their skills and dreaming of how, if we were lucky, one day we too might get sponsored by a manufacturer so we could cover some of the expense involved in replacing boards, trucks, wheels and shoes – and dedicate more time to what we loved.

Back in the village, conflicts with the police continued to escalate, and in order to bring an end to the ongoing confrontations we eventually came up with a plan to speak to the local politicians and ask them to provide a space where we could skate in peace. For several years we had been the only skaters in the village, but a group of younger kids had started to follow along, so we decided to make the most of the situation and collect signatures in order to petition for a spot to be designated for us.

Over the course of a year we attended various meetings with local politicians, who now promised to provide an area for us on the outskirts of town. We visited the location with them and they showed us several plans, asking for our advice and input. But even though they had the authority and it was at their discretion to see this through, in the end they never kept their word. We could deal with the letdown but the ongoing harassment from the local police under their orders only served to add insult to injury. For better or for worse, we were to gain first-hand insight into the intrinsic nature of those who triumph in politics.

* * *

On an exchange trip to France, when I was 13, I was caught in the company of a couple of girlfriends, smoking a joint in a toilet. It was the last night of our stay, and the locals had organised a farewell party for us in their village hall. I suspect that someone must have reported us, because the teachers came way out of their way to knock at our door, as if they already knew something was going on. Caught in the act, there was nothing much for me to say. But I'd be lying if I said I felt at all sorry for what I'd done.

As it was, I hadn't been the only one taking part in illicit activities that evening, but nevertheless I was to become the one the school made an example of. Upon our return to Spain I was questioned repeatedly by the headmistress and various members of staff, who wanted to know where the marijuana had come from. I didn't tell them, of course, that I'd snuck it across the border, and after many sessions of interrogating me and the girls I was with they were left with no choice but to give up on the matter.

The girls were soon let off the hook, and the headmistress, who considered that I was the main culprit who had led them astray, threatened to kick me out of school. In the end she relented, and over the following months I was kept in detention every afternoon instead, where I was given 'special' tasks intended to make me repent and lead me back to the light.

The incident led to further confrontation with my father, who once again threatened to kick me out of the house and have the authorities put me in a foster home if he found out I had been smoking again.

The next few years were rocky. My friends and I were linked to a series of graffiti paintings across the village, and when the school was broken into and sound equipment and computers stolen I was immediately put forward as a prime suspect and 'invited' to attend the local police station. Once there, I was questioned and told that if I didn't provide the information they wanted they would take it upon themselves to make sure I was incriminated. But in the end, due to a lack of evidence, the case was dropped.

During this period, my friends and I were regularly stopped by the police and searched without justification. Eventually we became tired of the ongoing harassment and decided to exact retribution. In the middle of a cold winter's night we set out to slash their tyres and rip the blue flashing lights from the roofs of their cars, the mere sight of which now caused an unpleasant fight or flight reaction in our guts. Over the weeks that followed, it brought us great joy to see the blue lights missing whenever they drove by.

Winters in the village were long and cold, so my friends and I resorted to hanging out in local bars, immersed in long sessions of alcohol consumption, table football and card games. Observing the colourful characters that inhabit these environments was, for me, a fascinating study in human behaviour. At weekends it wasn't unusual for us to get into some kind of altercation. Even though we weren't necessarily looking for trouble, we didn't need much provocation if anyone rubbed us up the wrong way. There is certainly enjoyment to be found in a good fight, especially if a man considers himself to be wronged, but in the end, what we put out always comes back, and while walking home late one night, Karma almost caught up with me when I was set upon by a bunch of older kids drugged out of their heads.

As I made my way home that evening, a packed car drove by, its horn blowing loudly as the occupants shouted through the open window. Every weekend there were fights with members of one village against another and I knew straight away that this group had made their way down from one of the neighbouring villages, were high on coke and looking for someone to beat up. Earlier that evening my friends and I were involved in a brawl with a group of people from their village, so I was on the lookout, knowing well that these were the moments when you could be caught off guard.

Suddenly I heard the car skid and abruptly change direction. They were coming back for me. Knowing I was in trouble, I began to run. The sound of the engine was growing louder and the headlights were about to pinpoint me on the pavement when I dropped down, just managing to hide behind a parked car.

Seconds later I heard the car stop. The doors opened as the occupants' footsteps rang on the ground. Crouching low, I set off again, throwing myself down behind some tall grass. By then I'd already reached my block and was only a short distance away from home. I knew that if I stayed where I was they'd eventually find me, so I took a chance, leapt to my feet and sprinted towards the front door as fast as I could.

The cry went up as they set off after me, armed and ready. Without looking back I ran for my life and, reaching for my keys, only just managed to get through the door in time, escaping by the skin of my teeth.

The next day I found out that one of my friends hadn't been so lucky. Hunted down by the same group later that night, he had been beaten with a steel bar and left badly injured.

* * *

Molly fell sick when I was fifteen.

She had more than made it through her near-death experience in France and lived to see another day, but her kidneys had been weak ever since, and they were now giving up completely. For three days she'd been vomiting blood. She looked old and frail, and was skinnier than ever. As I left for school the following morning, she lay under the palm trees panting rapidly. I stopped for a moment to stroke her soft, black fur for the last time.

While I was away, my father carried her to the local vet for her final injection. Molly had been like a sister to me: I had spent the greater part of my childhood with her by my side and would miss her greatly. Without her, the house felt empty. It took my father and me time to adjust to the loss, and to get used to life without her.

A few weeks later, I stepped out of the house one morning. At the end of the street, crouched behind a parked car, I spotted a stranger with a long telephoto lens pointing towards me.

My heart rate went through the roof. The adrenaline rush urged me to run over and smash the camera into his face. But before I even had the chance to move, something stopped me in my tracks. I knew better. They were protected by law. They could invade my privacy, but I didn't have the right to defend myself.

Never knowing when I might be followed, spied on, my phone tapped or my picture stolen disturbed me deeply over the years and I came to loathe the kind of people who could indulge in such unscrupulous behaviour. These were supposedly civilised individuals with university degrees who took it upon themselves to label my mother's killer an insane monster, yet their behaviour showed no signs of being any more civilised and was therefore all the more despicable. From the very beginning my mother's murder had received an unsurpassed level of press attention. The fact that my mother was an attractive white, blonde woman from a middle-class background and that the attack had taken place in broad daylight while she was walking with her small child in a wealthy neighbourhood provided all the juicy ingredients for a powerful headline story. And the fact that the killing remained unresolved for almost twenty years provided newspaper editors with yet another excuse to keep the story in the headlines and continue to promote an agenda of darkness and fear.

My last year at school was no less conflictive. By then, I was already counting the days until my sixteenth birthday, when I would finally be able to leave the education system behind and make my own decisions for myself.

Teachers preached to us that life was all about hard work and wasn't supposed to be fun. According to them, following our dreams was immature and foolish. Never were we taught to become self-reliant and independent or to believe that if we put our minds to it we could accomplish anything we wanted. The things that mattered to me were never talked about. What we are, why we are here, the true purpose of life – these things were all ignored while they moulded us instead all according to one pattern, fit only for the everyday grind from nine to five.

I was being sent out of class and kept back after school more frequently than ever; and it became the norm for my father to receive daily phone calls from the headmaster, threatening to expel me if my behaviour didn't change. Meanwhile there was constant conflict at home. While my father struggled with suicidal thoughts, all the tensions between us had reached boiling point and the slightest spark was enough to start a fire.

At the time I didn't always appreciate the personal trials my father was going through or how difficult it had been for him to raise me as a single parent all those years. My attention was absorbed in overcoming anything and everything standing in the way of my freedom and independence.

Sooner or later, a change had to come.

CHAPTER 15

A NEW REVELATION

'We refuse to believe that which we
don't understand.'

Napoleon Hill

I n September 2004, a month after my fifteenth birthday, my
father received a phone call from a senior police officer. Thir-
teen years had passed since my mother's murder, and although
I had no expectation that the case would ever be solved, my
father was patiently awaiting the overturn of the Double Jeopardy law.

Upon winning the election of 2001, the Labour Government
had promised that they would change this obsolete principle
which meant that a person couldn't be tried twice for the same
crime, not even if new and indisputable evidence was to be
uncovered. Since the collapse of the trial in 1994, the police had
continued to believe that Colin Stagg, the suspect acquitted,

was guilty of my mother's murder and that once the law was changed he could be tried for the second time and a conviction would be obtained.

My father and I had last flown over to England two years before, in the autumn of 2002, to provide new DNA samples. As usual, our visit had been brief, we couldn't take Molly with us and never liked leaving her at the kennels for too long. On this occasion we stayed with an old family friend who lived in the countryside near London.

A new team had been assigned to reassess the investigation and we were to meet them for the first time. I remember clearly the feeling of suspicion that overcame me during our visit to the original Scotland Yard, when one of the detectives took me aside and opened the door to a large room, walled with folders.

'Look …' he began. 'This entire room is dedicated to the investigation into your mother's murder,' he paused. 'So far it's been the most expensive and largest in British police history. It's a very important case for us and we're still working very hard to catch the man responsible.'

Before leaving, we wiped a swab against the inside of our mouths so that a DNA sample could be extracted to differentiate ours from that of the assailant.

I spent the next day with our family friend, while my father returned to Scotland Yard for a more in-depth briefing. The detectives explained to him that samples taken from my mother's body had recently been submitted to an independent forensic company and that tests had revealed the presence of two sets of DNA, one belonging to my mother and the other to an unknown male. The sample under examination, they said, showed strong signs of belonging to Colin Stagg, although

DNA technology was still not advanced enough to make an identification that could stand up in court. The investigation, he was told, was on hold until technology advanced enough to make a decisive match and the overturn of the Double Jeopardy principle had finally come into effect.

Two years on, as my father listened from our home in Spain to the officer at the other end of the line, he was given a shocking piece of information that threw everything we'd been led to believe out of the window.

Since our visit to Scotland Yard, the unknown male DNA sample had been comprehensively tested against that of Colin Stagg as well as several other suspects. In the end, however, the only profile that matched had not been Colin Stagg's, but that of a man named Robert Napper.

Further testing had been requested, but again the result was the same, and the likelihood of the profile being anyone other than Robert Napper's had been estimated at 1 in 12 million.

After all these years, this information seemed almost impossible for my father to process. Not only had the police never mentioned this name to us before, but they had already made similar sweeping assumptions about the possibility of anyone else being present on the Common that morning that could fit my description of the assailant. Now he was to learn, however, that the new suspect's physical description was almost identical to that of Colin Stagg.

But even if this was a freak example of the exception proving the rule, no trial could take place for the time being as a direct result of the police's failings in the investigation of the case. The Crown Prosecution Service would not accept the DNA results alone and insisted upon further testing and verification. The date of any trial, therefore, was postponed indefinitely.

The news of the latest suspect was of no great significance to me. Up until then, I had never been interested in knowing about any details relating to the case. When Colin Stagg was tried and released in 1994, while we were still living in France, my father had simply referred to him as 'the man the police consider responsible' and I had never attached a name to the person who killed my mother.

Whatever his true identity might be, as far as my father and I were concerned, any mistakes that the police might have made in the course of their investigation didn't amount to much more than sensational rumours being spread by the press. From the very beginning, the police had led us to believe that every aspect of the investigation had been carried out by the book. The truth was, however, that from the moment Robert Napper was first identified as my mother's assailant, the police were aware that, if it hadn't been for their mistakes, not only could my mother's murder have been avoided, but a staggering series of violent attacks on women could all have been prevented.

Although we wouldn't understand the full story until 2009, when a series of leaked documents would come into our possession, Robert Napper's name had been known to the authorities ever since birth because of his violent family background. Born in Erith, south-east London, and brought up in Plumstead, in his early childhood he was to witness his mother being repeatedly attacked by his father. When he was nine years old his parents ended their violent marriage and Napper was placed temporarily in foster care, along with his brothers and sister, where he was to receive ongoing psychiatric treatment.

Four years later, at the age of 13, he was sexually assaulted by a family friend on a camping holiday. The incident was to have a marked impact on his life, and in the weeks and months that followed he became obsessively tidy, reclusive and introverted. As time went by he began to bully his brothers and to spy on his naked sister – until by the time he was 18, unable to cope with his behaviour, his mother asked him to leave the house. In the years that followed, he found a succession of menial jobs, eventually working in a plastics factory, while continuing his psychiatric treatment.

As early as 1986 the name of Robert Napper had first become a matter of official police record when he was found, at the age of 20, in possession of an air weapon in a public area. Although he was cautioned, no fingerprints were retained and he received a conditional discharge.

Three years later, on 10 August 1989, a woman living next to Plumstead Common in South London was raped at knife point in her bedroom while her children played downstairs. After she reported the attack to the police, a DNA profile of the assailant was obtained.

A few weeks later Robert Napper confessed to his mother that he had raped a woman on Plumstead Common. So strong was the guilt he felt inside that prior to his confession he attempted to end his own life by taking an overdose. Faced with a moral dilemma, Robert Napper's mother decided to report the confession to the police, as well as to her son's psychiatrist, who also reported the event. Yet, on hearing this information, the police performed only a rudimentary check of the previous few days' notes, told her nothing had been reported and failed to investigate further. For reasons unknown, Napper was never spoken to in person, nor his arrest even considered.

Consequently, no DNA samples or fingerprints were taken and Robert Napper was not linked to the offence which would have resulted in a custodial sentence, preventing him from causing any further harm and stopping an entire chain of events in its tracks.

Over the following years a staggering number of sexual attacks of a rapidly escalating level of brutality took place in a small area of South London known as the 'Green Chain Walks'. On 10 March 1992 a woman was attacked from behind in an alleyway and sexually assaulted at knife point. After the attack was reported to the police, a DNA profile of her assailant was obtained.

Only eight days later another woman was assaulted, the assailant using a knife to control her and stabbing her breasts during the attack. Once again, the police were able to collect DNA from the semen left behind by her attacker.

Two months later, on 24 May, another woman was raped while pushing a buggy containing her two-year-old daughter. The assailant used a ligature, beating and punching her repeatedly. The DNA collected from semen left behind was sufficient to build up a genetic profile of the attacker, and matched that of the other two attacks. But Robert Napper was not formally identified, and these and all subsequent attacks could have been avoided if the police had only linked him to the offence against his first victim in 1989.

The so-called 'Green Chain Rapist' committed more than 100 sexual offences on as many as eighty women during the period 1989–94. To this day, most of the details of these cases remain buried – but all the evidence points to Robert Napper, and, ultimately, he is believed to be the man responsible for the series of attacks collectively known as the 'Green Chain Rapes'.

Almost five years after his first reported attack, in May 1994, Robert Napper was finally arrested and charged with the brutal murders of a young mother called Samantha Bisset and her daughter Jazmine. The following October, on trial at the Old Bailey, he pleaded guilty to manslaughter on the grounds of diminished responsibility, also pleading guilty to two counts of attempted rape and one of rape relating to the attacks taking place in the Green Chain Walks. In his summing up, the judge called Robert Napper one of the most dangerous criminals he had ever sentenced. Committed to Broadmoor high-security psychiatric hospital indefinitely, he was at last taken off the streets.

18 December 2008 was the date set for the trial at the Old Bailey. It had been more than sixteen years since the attack on the Common.

Ever since my mother's killer had been charged the previous year, reporters had been showing up regularly at our door. They wanted pictures, stories and any kind of dirt they could dig up. With Christmas approaching, the date of the trial was just around the corner, and as the intrusion reached its peak we found ourselves under the most intense scrutiny since the immediate weeks after my mother's passing. When I lifted the shutter from my bedroom window one morning, the opposite side of the street was occupied by a line of hired cars with waiting reporters. After all these years it seemed hard to believe that, with all that was going on in the world, somehow we were still front page news.

For weeks, they waited patiently from dusk to dawn, throwing their empty coffee cups and cigarette butts out of the open windows. When we refused to speak to them, they attempted to follow us everywhere we went, and after constantly ringing the door bell in vain they interrogated as many of our neighbours as they could, even pressuring a pregnant woman into telling them what she knew. By the way they approached her, carrying their aluminium flight cases, she had thought they were hardened criminals turning up at her door, armed and ready to resolve some long-running feud. As the days dragged by, I couldn't help but think that they might also be using some kind of surveillance equipment to monitor our conversations and that perhaps they had even tapped our phone lines as well.

For all these years we had managed to keep our identity secret, but with chaos unfolding on the block, our anonymity was becoming harder to maintain. Until then, only those closest to us had known anything about our past. Although my friends had always known that my mother had passed away, it wasn't until a few years before that I had shared with them the background to my story for the first time. They were shocked. At the time, the investigation into my mother's death remained unresolved and the suspect was still believed to be on the loose. But almost anyone who found out about the circumstances of my mother's death, and the fact that I had been the only witness, seemed to enter a state of shock.

* * *

I am certain that nothing in this life happens by accident. When I was 16 the book *Think and Grow Rich* had come into my hands. Written by Napoleon Hill in the 1920s, the principles presented were based on studies conducted under the guidance of Andrew Carnegie, one of the big American industrialists of his time, and included over 500 of the most successful men and women of that era – a long list, which included the likes of Henry Ford, Thomas Edison and Alexander Graham Bell.

Through his studies, Napoleon Hill came to a simple but powerful conclusion: the things we think about most, whether good or bad, inevitably end up manifesting themselves in our lives. As I first reflected on these principles, I remembered vividly a time when we were living in France and my father was teaching me to ride a bicycle along the length of the nearby canal.

'I don't want to fall in the water! I don't want to fall in the water!' I suddenly began to call out one morning. It was a cold winter day and the water was ominously muddy and dark. My father laughed, 'We always follow our attention. Forget about the water, just look at the path!' But so concerned was I that I would cycle off the edge that eventually, with a big splash, I did just that, disappearing into the icy cold waters. My father leaped forward as fast as he could and only just managed to grab me before I sank into the depths.

If we focus more on the things we don't want than those we want, we will inevitably draw them into our lives. Even though I was given proof of this at such an early age, it still took me many years to finally appreciate the power of this simple concept.

In Napoleon Hill's book, a particularly moving story was included, which resonated deeply with me. Doctors informed

Napoleon that his son Blair, born without ears, would be a deaf-mute for the rest of his life. According to them, this was simply one of those unfortunate cases in which nothing would make any difference. Yet Napoleon refused to accept the beliefs of these so-called experts, and instead he told them that, before he died, his son would live to have 100 per cent of his hearing, just like any other child.

Every single day, for the first four years of his life, Napoleon read to him the bedtime stories which he created to 'develop in him self-reliance, imagination, and a keen desire to hear', whilst at the same time turning the negative into a positive by establishing the empowering belief that his affliction was 'not a liability, but an asset of great value'.

At 18 months, Napoleon Hill realised that his son was beginning to hear, and by the time he was four years old he had already recovered 65 per cent of his normal audition. Years later, when his son was in college, a manufacturing company of hearing aids who had heard about his unusual case decided to build a mechanism that allowed him to recover the other 35 per cent of his hearing, just as his father had once predicted. Blair later went on to become an inspiration for hundreds and thousands of people who, without his help, would have been doomed forever after to a life without hearing or speaking.

As I reflected on this story and the principles referred to throughout the book, I was forced to look back on my life in a new light. Could it all be so simple? I wondered. People had always made all sorts of similar claims as to how I would turn out: that I would never talk again, that I would end up living under a bridge, or even repeat the same cycle of violence I had witnessed. I began to seriously question why some people consistently stumbled into difficulties and obstacles and encountered misery while others were able to enjoy the journey of life, remaining intact.

Was there a reason for my mother's death that went deeper than simply being in the wrong place at the wrong time? I wondered. I thought about her fear of being attacked from behind, the incident in the cinema and her dream of someone whose face she couldn't see killing her with a knife. Through my later studies in hypnosis I came to understand how the mind works. Our subconscious does not distinguish between vivid imagination and reality; when we repeatedly find ourselves immersed in vivid daydreams, reinforcing certain feelings and emotions on a regular basis, that's when the probability of manifesting a very similar scenario in 'real life' becomes strongest.

Over the years that followed, as I began to uncover the knowledge I sought, I promised myself that I would strive to leave all negativity behind and make a new start. I was certain I had seen the depths of darkness and was determined to learn the lessons that life had handed me so as to avoid stumbling unnecessarily over the same stone.

After leaving school at the age of 16, I had found a job in a local workshop, fixing cars in the afternoons while travelling to a nearby town in the mornings to attend formal classes. Two years later, at the age of 18, I had officially completed my apprenticeship and began working full time at a nearby garage.

It had been a heavy schedule, working long hours every week and taking care of my two-year-old bull terrier as well. But after all the years of conflicts at school I was living on my own terms and no longer obliged to fulfil anyone else's wishes or desires.

In my free time I travelled extensively to Barcelona, across the country and to different parts of Europe, seeing a long list of bands in concert, whilst digging for records through the crates of second-hand stores along the way.

As much as I loved cars, bikes and the craft of mechanics itself, the job had only ever been a means to an end – a stepping stone which provided me with a way out of school. Now the time had come to leave mechanics behind and pursue my passion for music instead. Not only was I tired of pouring blood and sweat into a job that lined someone else's pockets, but I began to feel trapped – because there was never enough time left in the day to dedicate to the things that were truly important to me. After all, one of the most valuable commodities in life is time – time to do what we love and spend with those we love.

Music has always played a very important part in my life. As a small child in France, we often went to a bar on the coast at the weekend, where a live band played cover versions. The musicians were friends of friends and often invited me up with them to join in with my cardboard guitar as they played some of my favourite songs.

Ever since my mother's death, along with nature's intrinsic beauty, music always provided a means for me to reconnect with the feminine. My mother had raised me on her favourite records by Marvin Gaye, Aretha Franklin, Anita Baker and Luther Vandross – and my father, who was a great music lover, always had an endless succession of jazz, blues, soul, reggae, funk, hiphop, flamenco, rock and classical records and tapes playing in the car. To this day, there is a long list of albums that take me straight back to our time in France, gazing out through our old Volvo's window, as I absorbed the beautiful scenery that surrounded us, and the music played on through the stereo.

Marvin Gaye's *What's Going On*, Jimi Hendrix's *Electric Ladyland*, Earth Wind and Fire's *That's the Way of the World*, Aretha Franklin's *Young, Gifted and Black*, Miles Davis's *Kind of Blue*, Dexter Gordon's *Our Man in Paris*, Thelonious Monk's Big Band and quartet, Paco de Lucía's *Entre Dos Aguas*, all the Bob Marley and the Wailers' recordings, and so many others.

At the end of my first year of work I had bought my first electric guitar, and although I had managed to figure out a lot by ear I wanted to fill in the gaps in my knowledge and decided to look for a music school that would focus on developing the skills necessary to become a working session musician. My research into the best music schools had led to the initial idea of travelling to the US to study, but the courses I wanted to attend began at an inconvenient time so I decided to move to London instead, and planned to arrive a few months after the trial.

A move back to London would, of course, involve the possibility of the press finding out about my whereabouts, but I had always been determined to live my life on my own terms and knew that it would be almost impossible for them, or anyone else for that matter, to know where I was going to be at any one time.

From a young age, I had somehow known that if a conviction was ever to be attained, I wouldn't be a witness to the unfolding of events. The idea of my mother's killer being condemned to a life behind bars brought me no great joy, and it is my belief that there will come a time in the near future where we will look back at the current prison system and mental institutions in the same way that we now look back on hanging, stoning and crucifixion.

There is a story in the Bible that I find particularly poignant, in which several rabbis discover a woman committing adultery. These so-called 'religious' men, who are about to stone her to death, bring her before Jesus. But just as they are about to inflict the punishment, Jesus kneels down and inscribes the following words in the sand:

Which one of you that is without sin; let him cast the first stone.

The four men immediately put their stones down, and Jesus – who was reported to be without sin and so could have stoned her, instead said, 'Woman, where are your accusers? Neither do I accuse you. Go and sin no more …'

As much as we would like to believe that the prison system's main objective is to help individuals reform, in reality it is the imposition of punishment designed to benefit others. Blinded by our suffering, those of us who have found ourselves on the receiving end of the equation too often use justice as an excuse, when really we are looking for the personal satisfaction of seeing somebody behind bars. Such satisfaction, however, I believe, is futile – and in my opinion, no one should ever be condemned to a life of incarceration without the opportunity of a second chance. We have all committed acts that have led to the suffering of other individuals, and I am undeniably guilty of such behaviour, even though I have received endless second chances. Is there really a fixed amount of time required for one to truly understand their lessons and repent for their actions?

I can't pinpoint exactly when I forgave my mother's killer. For me it was a process that happened gradually over time. Just as the nightmares faded when I was a child, in due time my feelings of negativity faded too. I was no longer the little boy who screwed up paper cutouts representing 'the bad man' and pounded them into the rubbish bin. I was an adult who could understand what had happened, why it had happened and why my mother's killer had done the things he had done. Organically I forgave my mother's killer long before he even had a name.

By the time I consciously forgave him, I could no longer recall any concrete individual, as such. His features had long since faded away and what remained was only part of a distant memory. I believe, however, that the very act of consciously accepting in its entirety all that life had handed me, and then of forgiving the person responsible, without condoning his behaviour in any way, allowed me the opportunity to let go of any unnecessary negativity I might have carried.

Much of the media and senior officers of the police have used names like 'monster' to describe my mother's killer. The actions of one man have undoubtedly affected the course of over eighty women's lives and through them many others – but it is my belief that the labelling of a person as a 'monster' is both a superficial and simplistic act which allows us to crucify that person while taking on a superior position for ourselves. It suggests that we are somehow inherently better, that if we had been in their shoes, a recipient of the same programming and experiences, somehow we would have acted differently. In the end, however, we are all a function of our own programming.

* * *

On the eve of the trial my father was due to fly to London. Out of loyalty to my mother he wished to attend. He considered that he had received more than enough second-hand information throughout the years, which only proved to be inaccurate and unreliable afterwards. This time he wanted to see things with his own eyes. Meanwhile, in order to avoid the escalating harassment of the press, a close friend came to collect me early one morning and with my bull terrier in the back seat we drove off secretly into the depths of the Pyrenees.

CHAPTER 16

THE PHONE CALL

'Character is what you do in the dark,
when you think no one is looking.'

Mark Cunningham

On 18 December 2008 Robert Napper pleaded guilty to my mother's killing at the Old Bailey, admitting manslaughter on the grounds of diminished responsibility. The trial was over within a day.

The judge, Mr Justice Griffith Williams, told him:

You stabbed her a total of 49 times and you even stabbed her when she was dead. All the while Alex was there. The marks of injury upon his face proved that at some time you almost certainly, in my judgement, dragged him away from his mother. Now, sixteen years or so later, in early adulthood, Alex knows the man who killed his mother has been brought, albeit belatedly, to justice. It may be that he can now close a long, drawn-out chapter in his life.

The conviction was based largely upon the strength of the DNA profile obtained from tapings taken from my mother's body, the red flecks of paint found in my hair that originated from a toolbox in Robert Napper's possession, as well as the footprint found on the Common that matched one of his shoes – both discovered during a search of his flat following his arrest in 1994.

During the trial, Robert Napper's psychiatrist informed the court that he was severely mentally ill, suffering from Asperger syndrome and paranoid schizophrenia. His barrister told the court about some of his diagnosed delusions:

> He was convinced he had an MA in mathematics, that he had received a Nobel Peace Prize, that he had medals from the time he was fighting in Angola, that he and his family were listed in *Who's Who*, that he had millions of pounds in a bank in Sidcup, that he and others could transmit their thoughts by telepathy … He also believed that he was kneecapped by the IRA and that he had his fingers blown off by an IRA parcel bomb but because he inhaled sparkle fumes this resulted in his fingers being miraculously repaired.

At the end of the proceedings, Mr Justice Griffith Williams concluded:

> You are in any view a very dangerous man. You still present a very high risk of sexual homicide, which can only be managed

in a high-security hospital ... You must be returned
immediately to Broadmoor ... I am satisfied there are sufficient
safeguards in place under the Mental Health Act to ensure
you will never be released unless you are no longer a danger
to the public ... That is highly unlikely to ever happen.

Before being taken down, Robert Napper volunteered an apology, which was read out by his lawyer and was directed to me personally, to my mother's family and friends and to Colin Stagg, the suspect the police had wrongfully arrested in 1994.

After the court proceedings were brought to an end, Assistant Commissioner John Yates – who later resigned from the force after his involvement in the *News of the World* phone hacking scandal – read the following statement to the press:

At last we can finally say that we have achieved justice for
Rachel Nickell and her family. We also acknowledge there are
other cases where more could and should have been done.
Had more been done, we would have been in a position to
have prevented this and other very serious attacks by Napper.
I particularly here refer to the dreadful murders of Samantha
and Jazmine Bisset in November 1993.

To Colin Stagg, he dedicated the following apology:

In August 1993, he was wrongly accused of Rachel's murder.
It is clear that he is completely innocent of any involvement in
that case. I today apologise to him for the mistakes that were
made in the early 1990s and we also recognise the huge and
lasting impact that this has had on his life and on behalf of the

Metropolitan Police today I have sent him a full written
apology.

Four months after the trial, I moved back to London. The city
which had once been my home had felt like just another foreign
place when I landed at Heathrow Airport with nothing but a
guitar and a small suitcase.

On the plane I had read Paulo Coelho's *The Alchemist*, a part-
ing gift from my girlfriend. They say home is where the heart
is, and as I travelled across town on the tube that day I felt as if
I were in two places at the same time. A bittersweet feeling
enveloped me as I found myself living out a parallel story to the
one contained in the novel's pages.

In the book, a young Andalusian shepherd called Santiago
embarks on his life's journey following a recurring dream
which tells him that he will find a hidden treasure if he travels
far away to distant lands and reaches the Egyptian pyramids.
Early in his journey, Santiago meets an old king, Melchizedek,
who encourages him to sell his flock of sheep so that he may
have the means with which to reach his destination. The king
insists that it is Santiago's duty to pursue his 'personal legend',
which he describes as being that which we have wanted to
accomplish from a very young age. Everyone, when they are
young, knows what their Personal Legend is, he tells Santiago,
and that when we are embarked on our true life's journey the
universe conspires in every way to help us fulfil our purpose.

While travelling through the Saharan desert, Santiago meets
a beautiful Arabian woman called Fatima and they fall deeply
in love. Santiago is tempted to put all his plans aside and settle
down with her. But as much as she longs to be with him, she

insists that she will only marry him after he finds his treasure. She will wait for him but will not allow him to stay because she understands that if he were to put his dreams aside to remain with her their happiness would only be temporary. Gradually she would lose respect for him and he would only be half a man, forever wondering what might have been and resenting the fact that he had failed to pursue his dreams.

Trials and tribulations await Santiago and he is to be robbed, beaten and kept hostage. But in time he comes to understand that it is not the destination which is most important but the knowing of one's path and that true love will not stop one's journey, for if it does, it is not true love.

A young woman called Anna had come into my life only weeks before my departure and we had fallen in love in the deepest of ways. In less than a month my life had been completely changed and as much as I knew for certain, just as Santiago did, that I should continue my journey and leave her behind, I had been greatly tempted to put my plans aside.

Our paths crossed for the first time several years before, when I stopped by her village on the way back from my mechanics classes. It was a warm, sunny day in early spring when I made my way to the bus stop and spotted her across the street, walking home from school. She was beautiful, with long dark curls that waved gracefully against her feminine silhouette and features that could easily have been those of a Saharan princess.

A few years later our paths crossed again when I was out with my friends at a gathering in a neighbouring village one warm summer evening. My hair, like hers, was long and curly and she had crept up on me from behind, to place a top hat on my head.

'You look like Slash!' she remarked coyly, referring to the lead guitarist of Guns N' Roses.

'Very funny!' I replied sarcastically, as I yanked the hat from my head and threw it across the crowd.

It was the last of our interactions that evening, but a mark had been left.

The following winter I was invited to a nearby village one evening and on the way we stopped to pick up some friends. I was sitting in the back seat of the car, when the door opened and Anna climbed in beside me. She smelt sweet, and although slightly nervous, I knew that she was pleased to see me again. That evening we finally introduced ourselves to one another for the first time and chatted for a short while – there was an undeniable electricity between us.

The following week my friends and I were due to travel to Barcelona for a concert, and at the last minute Anna ended up coming along. While driving her home later that night Anna and I immersed ourselves in conversation.

We talked about our views on life, my imminent move to London and our love of music. I was curious about her, so I began to ask about her dreams and ambitions.

Born under the sign of Cancer, from a young age her passion had always been athletics and her dream was to become a long-jump champion. Over the years, her father had accompanied her from meet to meet across the country, and they were very close. She had been ranked as high as third in Spain in her age group, but after suffering a recent knee injury she'd been forced to stop competing. Doctors had told her that she'd never be able to jump again and her dreams had, sadly, been put on hold. In the meantime, she'd become interested in physiotherapy and was considering pursuing a degree the following year. She also loved to sing and was part of a band with her older brother, who was the same age as me. Eventually, she wanted to have five children – another dream she had nurtured ever since she was a little girl.

It was the first deep conversation Anna and I shared together and as she began to open up, just like a rose blossoming before me, I began to see how truly beautiful she was. Absorbed in our conversation, the drive flew by.

As the journey came to an end, Anna gazed deeply into my eyes. 'Alex ...' she began innocently, 'if you found a woman you really liked, would you commit yourself to her completely?'

I knew that, however understated her tone, there was nothing hypothetical about her question.

'Of course,' I replied. 'We're all looking for that true, deep connection. But it has to be the right woman.'

As we pulled up in front of her house, I brought the car to a stop, leaned over and kissed her. 'I can't believe it!' she exclaimed as she opened the door and stepped out of the car, a beautiful smile on her face.

While I was away, Anna prepared a small diary for me, with a phrase for every day of the year describing how much she loved me and how much she missed me. 'Alex, you're the person who's treated me best in the whole world,' she often told me. There was no doubt in my mind that she was truly special and I was blessed to have her in my life.

I had been in London for a few weeks when, late one evening, I received a phone call from my father.

There was, he told me, some news he had to share. A series

of previously undisclosed documents had just come into his possession, leaked by officials from inside the Crown Prosecution Service. The files, he explained, revealed that the errors made by the police in the investigation into my mother's murder had been far more wide-ranging and damaging than we had previously been led to believe.

Although senior officers had admitted publicly to a handful of these mistakes at the time of the trial – most notably the failure to investigate the call made by Robert Napper's mother to the police in 1989, reporting his suicide attempt and confession to raping a woman – it now started to seem that unknown officers within the force had attempted to keep most of the information secret in what appeared to be a damage limitation exercise.

That night my father told me the full story of what had happened. As well as Robert Napper's background, the files included all the details, names, dates and events. From the other end of the line, I listened intently as, one by one, he began to read to me the catalogue of errors contained within the documents.

Following Robert Napper's first reported rape and the series of crimes that followed, a month before my mother's murder, in June 1992, 'Operation Eccleston' had been established, under the command of Detective Superintendent Landeryou, to investigate the series of attacks known as the 'Green Chain Rapes'.

The detectives had called upon the services of Paul Britton, the clinical psychologist later involved in the attempt to trap Colin Stagg into a confession. Paul Britton created a psychological profile of the assailant, which outlined that he was known to the police, lived, worked or went to school in the area bordered by the offences, was probably of low IQ or intellect and if employed was likely to be doing an intellectually undemanding job. He was also presumed to be suffering from various forms of sexual dysfunction and, given the increasing violence of his attacks, was likely to commit further offences and to kill.

The police noted that at no time did the assailant ever attempt to conceal his identity, allowing himself instead to be seen by his victims, often stalking and following them beforehand. He was capable of entering houses despite the presence of others and was not concerned by the presence of children, something that they reasoned brought increased excitement created by their proximity. His victims were also of a similar physical appearance, all of them physically attractive.

A month after the establishment of the 'Eccleston' operation into the 'Green Chain Rapes', I witnessed my mother's murder in a nearby part of town.

The investigation into her death, known as the 'Edzell Operation', was led by Senior Investigation Officer John Bassett (succeeded at a later date by Brian Younger) as well as deputy investigators Keith Pedder and Mike Wickerson.

As soon as the detectives from the Eccleston team were informed of the details of the case, its two senior officers contacted the Edzell team to let them know that in their opinion they were looking for the same man. But the Edzell team failed to grasp the similarities between the two investigations, and concluded instead that the cases were not linked in any way.

Six weeks after my mother's murder, on 25 August, a full police briefing on the 'Green Chain Rapes' was arranged for radio and press. The public broadcast included an e-fit image of the suspect compiled from descriptions given by his numerous victims. The response was immediate. A member of the public contacted the police to let them know that his neighbour Robert Napper lived in Plumstead and fitted the description of the assailant.

The information prompted Detective Constables Fell and Dunthorn to stop Robert Napper on his way to work on 28 August. Robert Napper offered to attend Eltham police station on 2 September to give a voluntary blood sample, but ultimately failed to attend. A letter was sent to him, asking him to attend on 8 September, but again he did not show up and his failure to attend and provide a sample was not followed up.

Meanwhile, only days after the report by his neighbour, Robert Napper was pointed out again, this time by a work colleague who identified the e-fit as 'Bob Napper'. But once again, the report was not followed up.

Three months after my mother's murder, on 27 October, Robert Napper was arrested after attempting to make copies of police headed notepaper in a photocopy shop. His home in Plumstead was searched and amongst the items found were a handgun, a crossbow bolt, a six-inch blade flick knife and a brown wood-handled lock knife with brass fittings. Not only had such a knife been described by the woman whose breasts had been stabbed during an attack, but its blade also matched the shape of the weapon established by the pathologist after examining my mother's wounds.

Also found during the search were 240 rounds of ammunition and the stolen gym membership card of a young blonde woman, inside an A–Z map on which her address was ringed.

Numerous locations were marked with handwritten notes like *'sodden filthy bitch'* and *'cling film on the legs'*. There were dots, crosses and other markings on and near the Green Chain Walks where specific attacks had been reported, including the woman whose breasts had been stabbed, and a mother who had been attacked while pushing her daughter's buggy. There were further markings on the area of ground directly adjacent to Wimbledon Common, confirming Robert Napper's awareness of the vicinity.

Robert Napper served a short period on remand and was sentenced to eight weeks in custody for the firearms offences. During his arrest, psychiatrist Dr Claire Roden visited him and informed the officers in charge that the public would be at great risk if Robert Napper was to be granted bail. But nevertheless he was released soon after, and no investigation took place of the disturbing and incriminating evidence found during the search of his flat.

Following his release, Robert Napper informed his own psychiatrist that he had been copying the police headed notepaper because he wanted an official document to obtain a .22 calibre pistol. The psychiatrist reported the information to the police, but once again Robert Napper was not apprehended.

A month after the honeytrap operation against Colin Stagg was launched, on 19 February 1993, two young boys found a biscuit tin buried on Plumstead Common, containing a .22 Mauser handgun and ammunition. Robert Napper's fingerprints were all over the tin. But despite his history of firearms offences and his psychiatrist's latest report, no action was taken by the police to apprehend him.

Later in the summer, on 31 July, only days before the conclu-
sion of the honeytrap operation against Colin Stagg, Robert
Napper was stopped by officers Special Constable Abbott and
WPC Gay, hiding in an alley after being reported stalking in a
road close to Plumstead Common, overlooked by woods on the
Green Chain Walk.

The officer's notes of Robert Napper's behaviour read:
'*Subject strange, abnormal, should be considered as a possible rapist,
indecency type suspect.*'

Robert Napper did not give a reasonable explanation for his
behaviour and was merely taken home and his conduct not
properly investigated.

While Colin Stagg was held on remand, during the night of
3 November 1993, a young woman named Samantha Bisset
and her three-year-old daughter Jazmine were brutally
murdered at their home in Plumstead. The investigation into
their death was known as the 'Bisset Inquiry'.

The post-mortem examinations were carried out by Dr Hill
and Dr Shepherd, the same pathologists who had examined my
mother's wounds.

Two months later, in January 1994, Robert Napper was
convicted of shoplifting. He was taken into police custody and,
once again, allowed to leave with no cross-checking of his prints
against other offences or crime scenes.

It would not be until early April 1994 that the police would
finally identify a fingerprint at the Bissets' home as belonging
to him. Arriving on the scene after the attack, the Metropolitan
Police Forensic Service had failed to take adequate prints from
Samantha's body, and wrongly eliminated some of Robert
Napper's fingerprints. Not only had their delay of five months

in identifying him allowed Robert Napper to commit further attacks, but shockingly, instead of arresting him immediately, the police allowed him to remain on the loose for another two months, during which time he was merely placed under surveillance and was observed by officers stalking other women on the sites marked inside his A–Z map.

It was not until 27 May 1994 that Robert Napper was finally arrested and DNA samples were taken from him for the first time, officially identifying him as the person responsible for the Bisset murders, as well as four of the Green Chain attacks. During his arrest, the four female victims were to pick him out at an identity parade, and although their cases would remain on file, more than thirty other women were invited to participate in video identification proceedings.

During a search of his home, two pairs of shoes and a red metal toolbox were seized. Not only did the shoe match the footprints found on the Common on the morning of my mother's attack but the toolbox matched the flecks of red paint found in my hair. The link, however, would take over a decade to be made.

Meanwhile, as the preparations for the trial against Colin Stagg took place, Senior Investigating Officer Mickey Banks, Detective Inspector Bryan Reeve and Detective Sergeant Alan Jackman of the Bisset Inquiry not only informed their superiors of the similarities between their case and my mother's but also spoke directly to the Edzell team regarding the similarities. Now retired, in a recorded interview Detective Inspector Bryan Reeve of the Bisset Inquiry recalled the circumstances:

We always believed Napper was Rachel Nickell's killer. It was difficult to accept when no one would listen to us at the time. The powers-that-be were convinced it was Stagg but there was no evidence. We had a man awaiting trial for the murder of Samantha Bisset and her daughter and we had established a link with the Green Chain rapes. He was a violent rapist and was a much better fit for Rachel's murder than Colin Stagg but nobody wanted to listen.

Sunday Express, 21 December 2008

Referring to a Detective Inspector attached to the Edzell team he said, 'I never blamed Keith Pedder, though. None of us did. He was under immense pressure from above to pursue Stagg.'

Along with the fact that Colin Stagg had been in prison at the time of the Bissets' murder, all the evidence pointed towards Robert Napper. The senior officers of the Edzell team were well aware that, if the case was taken to court, Colin Stagg might claim in his defence that Robert Napper was my mother's killer, not him. It seems, however, that the team's primary concern was to ensure instead that arguments about Robert Napper being my mother's killer didn't, as the police report said, 'cause problems with the Stagg trial'* rather than to investigate whether Napper had in fact been responsible.

Almost a year after the collapse of the trial against Colin Stagg, on 9 October 1995 Robert Napper pleaded guilty to the manslaughter of Samantha and Jazmine Bisset on the grounds of diminished responsibility. The evidence of his involvement

---

* Police report to CPS, 13 July 2004, para. 238.

in two attempted rapes and one rape relating to the Green Chain Rapes was also presented, to which he pleaded guilty. In the end, however, the prosecution did not present the evidence relating to his first attack of August 1989 prior to his suicide attempt. Allegedly, a contamination problem had arisen in the lab where the DNA evidence relating to that offence had been analysed and stored.

Ultimately, this explanation held little weight given that there were records of the report both his mother and his psychiatrist made to the police in 1989. Furthermore, following his arrest in May 1994, before his conviction was to take place, he had also made an incriminating comment about this attack, when his mother's witness statement was put to him: 'I have no comment to make, thank you … it is a long time ago, although I still remember some of the circumstances.'

As my father continued to share the information with me from the other end of the line, I couldn't help but wonder why all evidence relating to Robert Napper's first reported offence had not been submitted.

Two months later, on 20 December 1995, Robert Napper was interviewed in Broadmoor Secure Hospital regarding my mother's murder. During the questioning he denied ever going to Wimbledon and told the police he had probably taken leave from work the week my mother was killed.

His employment records showed that he had received a full week's pay, and officers failed to consider whether this was compatible with him going to Wimbledon Common on the day of the attack. The truth was that Robert Napper had been scheduled for psychiatric treatment on the morning of 15 July 1992, in an area of Wimbledon adjacent to the Common.

Furthermore, his A–Z map, then in the police's possession, also had markings adjacent to the Common.

Ultimately, however, it is believed that little, if any, investigation into my mother's death was undertaken between 1995 and 2001, due in part to the belief that Colin Stagg was responsible.

As my father finished outlining all of the information to me, the facts were overwhelming. In many ways, the leaked files only left more questions unanswered.

My mind drifted back, and I began to wonder why, in all these years, the police had never once made an official apology, either publicly or in writing to my family, Samantha and Jazmine Bisset's family, or to any of the numerous women who suffered from Robert Napper's violent attacks due to their incompetence. The conclusion of Robert Napper's trial for my mother's murder which had taken place only months before, it seemed, would have been the perfect time to bring closure to the case and apologise to all affected. Yet not only had the police chosen not to do so, but they had decided instead to apologise exclusively to Colin Stagg – who earlier in the year had already received an official apology for his wrongful imprisonment and a record compensation payment of over £700,000.

At the time of the trial, however, the leaked documents detailing the catalogue of errors made in the police's handling of the investigations relating to my mother's killer had not yet fallen into our hands, and the police had no reason to suspect that they ever would. Only Colin Stagg and his solicitor had any knowledge of these mistakes, and they had successfully used them as ammunition to help obtain his compensation payment.

I could only wonder, in going out of their way to apologise exclusively to Colin Stagg, and making a substantial payment to him alone, was the police offering a truly selfless gesture meant to compensate for the suffering he had endured as a direct result of their mistakes, or was the true motivation to keep him and his legal team happy so that they wouldn't reveal information to the public?

In the handling of the investigations into my mother's assailant, her murder, the 'Green Chain Rapes' and the killings of Samantha and Jazmine Bisset, there had been a catalogue of catastrophic mistakes that were subsequently covered up. Over the span of almost twenty years, not a single officer had ever been disciplined, but if the extent of the mistakes committed by the police became a matter of public knowledge it could lead not only to a public outcry for individual officers to be disciplined, but to the undermining of the police as a body. Given that the documents involved a catalogue of errors, and offences against over eighty women, the repercussions could be considerable.

Of all these questions, only one thing was certain: the 'white hats' from inside the system were so disgusted with the fact that the police were covering their tracks that they had decided to put their careers on the line by secretly passing over the documents to us in the hope that we would take the appropriate action.

As our call came to an end, my father had a request to make. Would I consider putting my name together with his in an action he was considering taking against the police? The idea was to bring all the mistakes to public light for the first time, and for the appropriate body to hold those responsible accountable, in the hope that lessons would be learnt, and vital errors like these could be avoided in the future.

'I need some time to think about it,' I replied. 'Let me think it over properly and get back to you.'

We said our goodbyes and I promised to call back the following week when I had reached a decision.

In truth I had little faith in an action of this nature ever achieving any kind of success. After all, the police were a self-regulating body and I knew the way they could exploit loopholes and employ creative ways to protect themselves if they so wished. There were so many questions to take into consideration. Could we really set a precedent or achieve any type of meaningful change? I wondered. What would be the cost, both emotionally and financially? And what toll would this take upon my father after all these years?

My first days in London had been quiet. The child who was once the most famous in Britain was now unrecognisable to the outside world. My voice was deep, my body was that of an adult and my features were those of a foreigner. Ever since my return, my life had come full circle in more ways than expected.

Only days after my arrival, I met with my uncles Mohan and Chan for dinner one evening. During our time in France a dispute had arisen between my father and my grandmother, which had led to a rift. There had been no communication between us since, but over time the elder of my uncles had started writing to my father and we had kept in contact ever since. He was now helping me with the paperwork I needed to rent a place of my own, and in the meantime I was staying with friends on the other side of town.

One sunny afternoon towards the end of April, while sharing some drinks beside the Thames, my uncle suggested that I come and visit my grandmother and her husband. 'Just come and have lunch at the house,' he suggested. 'She would love to see you.'

Until then, the idea of re-establishing old ties, visiting our old flat or going back to Wimbledon Common hadn't even crossed my mind. Since my arrival, my attention had been focused entirely upon my studies.

'Let me think about it and get back to you,' I replied.

A few days later I gave him a call and agreed to meet the following weekend near my grandmother's in North London. If it hadn't been for my uncle the opportunity would never have presented itself, and I felt certain that the timing was right, and that everything was happening for a reason.

Even though I still had memories of my grandmother, after all these years it would almost be like meeting someone new. They still lived in the same house in which we had spent the weeks following my mother's death, and while we sat eating lunch in the garden in which I had picked the rose with my father so many years before, my grandmother and her husband invited me to come and stay with them, rather than renting a place of my own.

Over the next week I thought their offer through. The visit had left me with a good impression and, ultimately, I concluded that there was something to be gained by everyone. If things didn't work out I could always leave, knowing that at least I'd given the situation a fair chance. Most importantly, even though there was still an enormous chasm of misunderstanding between them, by making that first step I felt that the process of bringing my grandmother and my father together again had begun. I had been dazzled during that first visit by the striking resemblance between their eyes.

The following week, I phoned my father to let him know how everything had transpired. He listened quietly as I explained that if he ever wanted me to speak to his mother on his behalf, I would be more than happy to do so.

Later on, he would tell me that this had been a watershed moment in his life. No one had offered to help resolve any family dispute for him before, and it struck him that his responsibilities as a father were coming to an end.

During the weeks that followed, my grandmother and I talked regularly and began to discover more and more about each other. While discussing the smallest of subjects, we could naturally find ourselves evolving into a much deeper conversation.

Even though the relationship between my father and her husband had been difficult, they were both helpful and supportive during my stay, going out of their way to make sure my needs were met.

The next time my father and I spoke, I told him I would be glad to put my name alongside his in the action to expose the police. He had done so much for me throughout the years that it was only right for me to stand beside him. In consideration of all the women who had suffered at the hands of my mother's killer as a direct result of the police's failure to protect them, we felt it our duty to do all we could to bring the files secretly handed over to us to public light for the first time.

CHAPTER 17

JUSTICE?

'Things do not change; we change.'

Henry David Thoreau

At the end of January 2010 I returned to Spain after my year in London.

Only weeks after my arrival, my father suddenly began to complain of an intense jolt of electricity striking the side of his temple. Over the following months, the pain, which he compared to being hit around the face with a baseball bat, began to recur at the most random of times, often lasting up to twenty minutes on end. These jolts were so intense that my father could hardly bear them. During these episodes he walked around in circles, stooped over with his head between his hands, praying that the pain would somehow fade away.

As the days went by, the pain became more frequent and my father began to spend more and more time on his own, lying in bed with the lights out and a bag of ice pressed against his face. One evening he came to me in tears. He was in great distress and had become so sensitive that he couldn't even bear the sound of a far-off neighbour's dog barking. He complained that the vibration was aggravating the pain to a level which he simply couldn't stand.

I ran out into the street and, hanging over the neighbour's fence, I did my best to calm their frantic dog. Eventually he began to quiet down and I returned to the house to check on my father. He was clearly exhausted. The strains of life were taking their toll. For almost twenty years he had been a single parent, always doing his best to fulfil my needs, while at the same time dealing with the stress of family rifts, an ongoing police investigation and unscrupulous press intrusion which had led us to flee and to hide, first in France and then in Spain.

In the months leading up to my return, our solicitor, Kate Maynard of Hickman & Rose, had written to the Chairperson of the Independent Police Complaints Commission (IPCC) informing him of our complaint, which sought to make the mistakes detailed in the leaked files a matter of public record. The letter was sent on 16 November 2009, accompanied by an indexed lever-arched file of meticulously compiled documents, based largely on those handed to us from inside the CPS.

In making this complaint, she wrote that her client was seeking the following:

Acknowledgment of and explanation for the serious failures of the MPS in the three investigations. To bring officers to account for those failures, including the bringing of disciplinary proceedings where appropriate. To ensure that lessons are learned, so that other families will not suffer as theirs has done from such grave police failures.

Solicitor Kate Maynard of Hickman and Rose,
letter of complaint to IPCC, 16 November 2009

The following summer, on 3 June 2010, the IPCC's report was made public. The main conclusions read as follows:

Throughout the investigations into the Green Chain rapes and Rachel Nickell's murder there were a catalogue of bad decisions and errors made by the MPS as outlined in this report. Without these errors, Robert Napper could have been off the streets before he killed Rachel Nickell and the Bissets, and before numerous women suffered violent sexual attacks at his hands.

When Napper was convicted in 2008, Assistant Commissioner John Yates publicly apologised to Colin Stagg for the miscarriage of justice. However, nobody at the MPS has ever stood up in public and offered an apology to the other people whose lives were so terribly affected by this case.

In all these circumstances, I have concluded that the most appropriate and effective next steps need to focus on a public apology and acknowledgment of failings together with detailed evidence of learning and improved practice by the Metropolitan Police Service.

IPCC Commissioner's Report on Hanscombe's complaint,
June 2010

A few days later we received a letter from Cressida Dick, Assistant Commissioner of the Metropolitan Police.

Dear Mr Hanscombe,

I am writing to you as the Assistant Commissioner in charge
of homicide and other serious crime investigations in the
Metropolitan Police Service (MPS). I have considered the
IPCC report about the complaint made by you regarding the
investigations into the death of Rachel, the Green Chain rapes
and the deaths of Samantha and Jazmine Bisset. The MPS
has publicly accepted the findings of the IPCC report and its
recommendation.

I understand that on the day that Robert Napper was
sentenced, Assistant Commissioner John Yates met with you
and apologised unreservedly for the missed opportunities and
mistakes made during the investigations into Rachel's murder
and the police contact with Robert Napper. On behalf of the
MPS I would like to repeat to both of you and Alex the
unreserved apology for the failings that have occurred. I am
extremely sorry for the mistakes that were made. In making
this apology I acknowledge the huge and devastating impact
that the tragic death of Rachel has had on your lives.

The Metropolitan Police Service has publicly acknowledged
that more should have been done and we could have been in
a better position to have prevented the dreadful attacks by
Robert Napper, including Rachel's death.

I would like to reassure you that the systems and structure
of major investigations today greatly reduce the potential for
such errors to occur again.

If you would like to meet with me then I would be very
willing to do so.

Yours sincerely, Cressida Dick
Assistant Commissioner, Metropolitan Police

Our claim to the IPCC had been a success. We now held in our hands the first official apology we had ever received from the police.

But in spite of this concession, not only did the police fail to apologise to any of the other women but they also refused to fulfil any of the IPCC's recommendations. Their reassurance that things had now changed was not the comprehensive demonstration that they had been ordered to provide. To us, it was only an empty promise. After all, the mistakes made throughout the three investigations had never been due to a lack of technology but a product of human error and lack of managerial oversight.

The fact that the Chairperson of the IPCC, with the full power of the state behind her, could not oblige the police to follow her recommendations not only proved that the IPCC was a toothless tiger with no power to enforce its own rulings but served to underline the simple fact that, in the UK, the police were not truly accountable to anyone – protected by the blanket shield of immunity provided by the Hill Ruling.

The previous summer, at the very beginning of the process, our solicitor had explained to us that although the leaked files were absolutely damning, our chances of achieving any kind of positive outcome were slim. Apparently, this all boiled down to one major point: in the UK police officers were exempt from the consequences of their incompetence or malpractice. The Hill Ruling made in the House of Lords in 1989 had set a precedent that meant that the body employed to ensure that the 'common people' face the consequences of their actions was itself exempt from such responsibility simply because, according to the ruling, they were 'well intentioned'.

In the handling of the investigations into my mother's assailant, her murder, the 'Green Chain Rapes' and the killings of Samantha and Jazmine Bisset, there had been a catalogue of catastrophic mistakes that were subsequently covered up. In my eyes this seemed to demonstrate that, although there are many well-intentioned and diligent police officers in the force, there are also those who are not and that a system exempt of liability leads to increased corruption – because weak people are drawn to positions in which they are not obliged to be accountable for their actions.

Doctors, after all, are also well intentioned, but when mistakes happen the UK courts still force them to take full responsibility for the consequences of their actions. Not only are doctors obliged to compensate those who have suffered from their mistakes but, depending on the degree of their incompetence, they can also face criminal proceedings. But even though a surgeon has people's lives in his hands every working day, the law does not accept that this will lead him to exercise his function in a detrimentally defensive frame of mind. In reality, the fact that an individual is held responsible for their mistakes only attracts a more competent person to such a position in the first place.

And so my father and I were faced with a decision: either we could walk away now, having achieved the acknowledgement and apology we had sought, or we could take one final step and attempt to set a precedent that could eventually lead to the scrapping of the Hill Ruling.

If we decided to continue, there were three avenues available to us.

Our first option, a public inquiry, would take place within

the boundaries of the UK, and was the most powerful way of bringing about change. The inquiry's chairperson would be able to make strong recommendations to Parliament which could lead to a change in the law, something that had already been demonstrated in the case of Stephen Lawrence, a black teenager killed in a racially motivated attack in South London in 1993, where a public inquiry had led to the scrapping of the 'Double Jeopardy' principle.

For us, however, this option was already out of the question. While preparing the documentation to accompany our claim to the IPCC, our solicitor had contacted the three victims of Robert Napper's 'Green Chain' attacks whose cases were successfully prosecuted in 1995, along with that of his first victim whose case was bungled. The idea had been to invite them to join in with our complaint, so that their cases could be addressed individually. In spite of the fact that by taking part they would be put in the public spotlight and possibly suffer the negative stigma of having been subjected to these attacks, two of the women were courageous enough to join us almost imme-diately and the other two agreed to consider the possibility. But upon hearing this, officers from the police had allegedly contacted the four women and 'suggested' to them that taking part in our claim was not a good idea and soon after they all withdrew their support.

Without the participation of any of Robert Napper's other victims, not only were we unable to address their individual cases in our claim to the IPCC, but it was no longer viable for us to press for a public inquiry.

The second option involved taking our claim to the European Court of Human Rights (ECHR), where it would be heard outside the boundaries of the UK. There were no guarantees, but if successful our claim could force the police to make a symbolic compensation payment to our family. Although this would not lead to a direct change in the law, by setting a precedent it could eventually lead to the scrapping of the Hill Ruling.

The third option went straight to the point and involved sidestepping the ECHR completely and instead asking the police directly to reimburse the costs involved in preparing our claim to the IPCC – which had acknowledged that without their mistakes my mother's death could have been avoided – and by asking for a symbolic offer of compensation. Such a payment, even to the value of £1, would set a precedent, not only making any claim made by Robert Napper's other victims far more likely to succeed but, most importantly, making any unrelated future claims by members of the public for police negligence much more likely to succeed, which potentially could lead to the scrapping of the Hill Ruling altogether.

After twenty years of involvement in police investigations and legal wrangling, my father and I decided that we would make a final attempt to do what was in our hands to set that precedent. By asking the police directly for what was morally right, we would allow them the opportunity to show genuine goodwill and take responsibility for their actions without being forced to do so by an independent body.

The following month, in July 2010, our solicitor went ahead with our plan by replying to Assistant Commissioner Cressida Dick, asking for the return of our legal costs incurred in preparing our complaint to the IPCC, and a symbolic offer of compensation.

A month later, the police still hadn't replied, so on 17 August 2010 our solicitor filed an application to appeal at the European Court of Human Rights (ECHR) on our behalf. Although we didn't necessarily have the intention of seeing this through, given the strength of our case there was still a possibility that a verdict favouring us could be reached if we went ahead, and filing the paperwork served to maintain pressure on the police.

On 28 September 2010, two months after our solicitor's letter, we received a reply, this time from Assistant Commissioner Cressida Dick's solicitor.

Dear Sirs,

Re: Andre & Alex Hanscombe

I write in substantive response to your letter dated 5th July 2010, which sought confirmation as to whether my client was prepared to offer compensation to your clients as a gesture of goodwill, and for them to reimburse their reasonable legal costs of pursuing the police complaint. These costs, which I note include your costs of pursuing an application to the ECHR and a success fee, are in excess of £53,000.

The Metropolitan Police Service is a public body that is accountable to the taxpayer. In this case, my client has no legal liability to your clients, which you have accepted in your 5th July letter. Moreover, the failings in the investigation have publicly been acknowledged and my client has apologised unreservedly to your clients for this, both before and after the IPCC investigation.

Taking all these factors into consideration, and having reviewed your request in detail, I am instructed that my client is not prepared either to compensate your clients or pay their legal costs.

Although it will not affect the decision, if your clients would still like to meet with Assistant Commissioner Cressida Dick, she would be very happy to do so.

Yours faithfully, Andy Fairbrother

Directorate of Legal Services, Metropolitan Police

From the time it took for the police to reply to our letter, it was clear that their decision had not been made on impulse, but after much thought and consideration. In their letter, their solicitor made clear that the police had no intention of doing what was morally right and had chosen once again to hide behind their blanket shield of immunity provided by the Hill Ruling. The letter also seemed to suggest that, because an apology had been made, the police had exempted themselves from any and all responsibility. Why then had they chosen to make a significant payment to Colin Stagg? Wouldn't an apology have been sufficient? At the trial at the Old Bailey, Robert Napper had also volunteered an apology to us for taking my mother's life. It was clear, however, that he would still have to take responsibility and face the penalty for his actions – the police themselves had labelled this 'justice'.

Their solicitor also seemed to imply that, because the MPS was a public body accountable to the taxpayer, they had a limited budget and therefore had to set priorities.

In 1994, long before any of the police mistakes had come to light, my family had received £97,000 from a state-run body called the Criminal Injuries Board for the loss of my mother's services. This payment, although originating from the taxpayer, had nothing to do with the police, and therefore did not set any type of precedent. Given that Colin Stagg had received his payment of £700,000 for serving ten months in prison in 1994, it appeared that his circumstances were calculated to be of much greater significance than my mother's life.

There had already been similar occasions where the police had used taxpayer money to compensate victims of crime for their incompetence. Following the death of Stephen Lawrence the police had made a payment of £320,000 to his family for the delay in apprehending his assailants, even though the attack was not due to their mistakes – and it was only their lack of professionalism which had led to a delay of seven years in convicting his attackers.

Why, then, would the police make a payment to Stephen Lawrence's family and refuse to even reimburse our legal costs? In my mother's case, not only had the failure of the police to apprehend Robert Napper led to her murder, but due to their lack of professionalism there was a further delay of sixteen years between her death and the time of his conviction – more than twice the time it took in the Lawrence case. Many argued that the underlying reason behind the payment in the Lawrence case was not necessarily because the police wished to put things right but instead because they were being condemned as 'institutionally racist' and they hoped that making such a payment would help clean up their public image.

I was, of course, never in a position to say who should receive what. The disparities, however, were endless, and I could only conclude that the decisions made by the police were either entirely random or that their choice to make payments to Colin Stagg and to Stephen Lawrence's family was simply because their cases did not create any kind of precedent for police negligence. Yet my mother's case, which was one of the largest investigations to take place in the UK, involved numerous women who suffered at the hands of Robert Napper because of the direct mistakes of the police – and they feared that making any kind of payment to us would set a direct precedent.

In an investigation which had affected over eighty women the floodgates could be opened to an avalanche of claims, and if the scrapping of the Hill Ruling was ultimately to take place, an irresistible pressure to discipline the officers involved could develop. The repercussions on a nationwide scale would be immense.

In December 2010 my father and I decided to withdraw our claim to the ECHR. Our attempt to pressure the police into setting a precedent had been unsuccessful.

Although it hadn't necessarily been our intention to continue to the bitter end, the hearing originally expected to take place within eighteen months had recently been postponed indefinitely, and I interpreted it as a sign. We had played our cards as best we could and it was now time to step aside.

Meanwhile, my father's health was deteriorating and I believed that, after so many years fighting on so many different fronts, another protracted legal battle would only be detrimental. His well-being and recovery were to me the main priorities. Sometimes, in order to win the war, you have to sacrifice the battle.

Quietly, comforted in the certainty that every decision we had made had been the right one and that, equally, it was now time to step aside, we brought an end to our claim and, together, we turned the page on a chapter of our lives which had lasted over two decades. In the end, we couldn't dictate the standards under which other people lived their lives, only how we chose to live ours.

Ultimately, no one can escape their karma. Eventually, one way or another, we will all face the consequences of our own actions.

CHAPTER 18

A NEW BEGINNING

'You must never be fearful about what you are
doing when it is right.'

Rosa Parks

O ver the years I had become interested in handwriting analysis. Also known as graphology, this science is held in high regard by major corporations, due to its accuracy and ability to reveal personal traits. In many cases it is an indispensable tool in the selection of new employees for senior positions.

The act of writing is not a conscious one: we just hold the thought we wish to communicate in our mind and the subconscious automatically takes over, producing a script that reveals personality characteristics that are invisible to the untrained eye, so that information that could take many years to discover by other means is available on paper as soon as someone writes a few lines.

One day I decided to look at some letters my mother wrote before I was born.

Her handwriting revealed a number of positive traits, most noticeably a fast mind, kindness and a good sense of humour. But there were also a number of negative traits such as resentment, pessimism and a tendency to live very much in the moment, without planning ahead. The most significant trait of all, however, was low self-esteem or a lack of self-love.

As I looked at her handwriting, I couldn't help but notice how precisely these traits tied in with the struggles she had faced throughout her life. On her hip she carried a scar that came from a violent episode with an old boyfriend. 'I always told myself that if anyone hit me I would never go back,' she had explained to my father, but after the incident she had been unable to keep the promise she had made to herself and the scar became a reminder of the shame she felt inside.

A few months after my birth my mother had begun to notice that the more happiness she experienced with 'her little pack', as she used to call us, the worse she felt about herself. This dichotomy caused her great distress and confusion.

At these moments, my father often reminded her that she was bright, outgoing, well-read, dynamic and intelligent – and that she possessed bucketfuls of enthusiasm and charm. But my mother didn't feel this herself and anything my father might have said left her almost completely unmoved. No matter how much joy we might have brought her or what my father did in an attempt to make her happy, my mother felt troubled. Eventually my father suggested that she write down on paper everything that was disturbing her as this might help to pinpoint the cause of her distress.

But no matter how hard my mother tried she was unable get the words onto the page – something which only served to increase the frustration she already felt. Not being capable of understanding why she was so unhappy, she had come to the conclusion that she needed professional assistance and she began seeking out a competent psychologist, although in the end she was never to see this through before her death.

I couldn't help but see a pattern, connecting my mother's life with that of her killer. No matter how hard it may be to accept, in life we don't get what we want. Neither do we get what we need. We only get that which we believe we deserve.

One of the detectives involved in the investigation into the crimes committed by Robert Napper once described him as 'a culmination that was feared by both professionals and lay observers'. Years later, at the time of his conviction in 2008, the judge described him as 'a very dangerous man'.

As I reflected and imagined myself in his shoes I could see clearly that in the end we are all merely a function of our programming. Like many others, my mother's killer was a man who had been dealt a bad hand. His adult choices were a direct result of his formative experiences as a child, and there is no doubt that, because of the lack of the love and guidance he would have needed to overcome the bad programming he received, he went on to perpetuate the subsequent fatal cycle of violence.

I have nothing but gratitude for the decision my father once made to take me away from the influence of psychologists and psychiatrists, no matter how well intentioned their efforts. It was his love and dedication that allowed me to recover my balance. I have always wondered if, had I been left in the care of psychologists, had I been prescribed psychiatric drugs over the years, would I have repeated the same cycle of evil to which I had been exposed? Perhaps it's only due to my father's foresight and understanding that my story did not take a very different course altogether.

In spite of the difficulties both my parents encountered in their formative years, they understood the power of love. Thanks to all the love, guidance and support my parents gave me I have always held myself in high regard. Despite the fact that I was to lose my mother at an early age, I have always felt in many ways more privileged than many. What she gave to me, nothing and nobody can ever take away. That is the power of unconditional love.

While my father was sick I made sure to be there and care for him. Despite being a strong advocate of avoiding conventional medicine for most of his life, as his health deteriorated and the illness worsened, the pain was becoming so unbearable that at night he could no longer sleep. A dynamic was beginning to develop, in which out of desperation he felt forced to accept painkilling injections at the local hospital in the early hours of the morning.

At first I struggled to understand the pain he was feeling, but over the course of several months the doctors eventually discovered that the jolts of electricity were emanating from the trigeminal nerve. Often referred to as 'suicide disease', the condition he was suffering from has been described as one of the most painful known to mankind. The unpredictable jolts of electricity can become so unbearable as to push sufferers over the edge, leading them to take drastic measures. As a general rule doctors prescribe heavy painkillers and anti-depressants as treatment.

Many have undergone radical surgeries, only to find the pain return, so it was a godsend when a friend recommended to us the use of 'apitherapy', a treatment used by the ancient Egyptians that involved the medicinal use of bee stings administered to strategic points of the patient's body. Mellitin, an active agent found in the venom of the bee, has 100 times the strength of cortisone, a steroid often used as an anti-inflammatory in modern medicine.

After only a few sessions, the pain was never to return. In hindsight, and once my father had been able to sleep and recover for the first time in months, he concluded that the detonator for all the pain he had experienced over the course of that year had not been physical, but emotional. Now that I had matured into an adult and his responsibilities as a father were coming to an end, he had finally allowed himself to start letting go of all the pain he'd been holding on to for so many years.

Over the weeks that followed we were to reflect deeply upon all the struggles, disagreements and conflicts between us since my mother's passing. We both knew things could have been done better, if we had known then what we knew now.

Around this time, Anna and I decided to part ways. We'd been together for several years and had reached a fork in the road. From the moment we met, our lives had been bound tightly together. We loved each other in the deepest of ways and had shared some of the most beautiful moments of our lives together. Recently, however, we had found ourselves growing apart. 'In another time and place where things work differently, if it is meant to be our paths will cross again,' we had finally agreed.

In the summer of 2011 I decided to leave Spain again and was planning a trip to South America, where I intended to stay on, eventually making my way towards Asia.

Before my departure, Anna and I were to meet one last time. Nothing had changed in the love we felt for each other. We had seen each other again over the past months, and as much as we enjoyed our time together there was always a bittersweet feeling. The beauty and sadness of the moment had brought her to tears each time. She said that for her it felt as if time had stood still and that she needed me to be on the other side of the world to be able to continue her life without me.

As I drove down to her house that late summer afternoon, I couldn't help but notice how stunning the scenery around me looked. Endless fields, mountains and forests. There was no doubt in my mind that this was a beautiful part of the world. The sky was a clear blue and the warmth of the August sun on my tanned skin felt just right as the breeze blew through the window, and the music sounded softly through the car's speakers.

That day we drove for endless miles, cruising towards the French border along open country roads, before finally settling on a deserted, unspoiled beach. As we lay together on the sand, with the sun setting above us, we could both feel how special this part of our lives had been for each of us.

Driving back towards home late that night, Anna fell into a deep, peaceful sleep beside me. I glanced towards her out of the corner of my eye and treasured the moment. She looked incredibly beautiful.

Moments later, we stood together in the dark at the bottom of her street. 'I want you to know that no matter what happens you will always be strong and smart, beautiful and feminine …' I paused for a moment, as I stroked her hair. 'I want you to know that whenever you are feeling less than perfect, whenever things aren't going the way you wanted or expected them to go, you can always find me here …' I pressed my palm against her solar plexus, '… in that special place. I will always be there, deep inside you.' Her eyes were wet with tears. I held her tightly in my arms, as I reassured her, 'Everything will be OK,' and kissed her for the last time.

From time to time, she appears in my dreams. I know that one day, in one way or another, no matter how briefly, our paths will cross again.

EPILOGUE

On a recent visit to London I returned to Wimbledon Common. Twenty-three years had passed from the day I watched my mother's soul leave her body, and never before had I ever felt the need, or the slightest desire, to return – but, for some reason, the time had come. I wanted to see whether I recognised anything or if the scenery triggered a special response within me.

On a cold January afternoon I set off down to the station from my grandmother's home in North London to catch the tube across town. During the journey I sat gazing thoughtfully through the window, and as the sun shone gently in my eyes and I took in the passing city landscape, I reflected back on everything that had transpired since I'd left Spain four years before. For the first time since our rift, when I was eight, I had made contact with my maternal grandparents and we'd begun exchanging letters – and for the first time in over twenty years my father had met up with his mother.

As the wagon descended underground and the light faded, I remembered a dream I'd recently had. For the last four years

I'd been travelling the world. I'd been exposed to different cultures, different landscapes and different faces. For much of the time I'd been in India studying yoga with my teacher R. Sharath. It was then that I awoke suddenly in the middle of the night with a feeling of complete clarity. My dream had many layers and I could perceive sights and sounds way beyond the realms of my normal senses. There were groups of spirits who had been assigned the role of influencing humanity in opposing ways, and even though some were influencing us to take part in evil deeds and others were influencing us to be righteous, they were all equally advanced and intelligent beings. They were also equally virtuous, and couldn't be described as either good or bad. Just as in a film, they were simply fulfilling the role which had been assigned to them by a higher power, with no attachment or emotion whatsoever.

In my dream I was able to interact with these spirits at work while the rest of humanity continued with their lives, totally unaware of our presence.

The spirits that were there to guide and support us transmitted to me the message that we are all spiritual beings having a temporary material existence, and in the process have forgotten what we truly are. Wordlessly, they explained that, whatever situation I might be faced with, the 'bad deeds' of another person could only have a negative impact on me if I forgot that they were there for a reason, and that they presented a lesson. I could choose to react negatively, but if I stayed stable, simply observing them, like the changing of the seasons, they would have no negative effect whatsoever upon me and would instead propel me forwards faster than I could ever imagine.

In my twenty-five years of life I had never been visited by a light, at least that I could recall, but I was left with no doubt in my mind, upon awakening, that – wherever it had come from – the message I had received was incredibly powerful.

Wimbledon – last stop on the line.

Finally, I had arrived. I stepped down from the carriage, climbed up the stairs, reached for the card in my pocket and made my way through the exit. As I walked out onto the street, I stopped for a moment to look around. Nothing seemed particularly familiar, nothing stood out in any way. It was just another busy high street, with just another group of people going about their everyday lives.

I looked at my watch. Half past three. There was only so much time before sunset. Stepping into a local newsagent's, I asked for directions to the Common. 'I'm sorry, I've never been there,' came the reply. I stepped into the dry cleaner next door. Same response. How could they live so near and never have been there?

Perhaps it was just a coincidence, but I interpreted their lack of guidance as a sign that I should find my own way; a reminder to use my intuition. I turned and walked up the street, eventually passing a sign that confirmed I was heading in the right direction. As I entered a noticeably wealthier area, there was a sudden change of energy, sights and scenery. But still, nothing stood out in my mind as being particularly familiar.

I continued along the pavement, passing people walking their dogs. Now I knew I was near. As I made my way up the hill I began to see greenery and trees in the distance. Soon, I reached the edge of the Common. All of a sudden, a strong feeling of going home overcame me. The passers-by couldn't possibly recognise me, but in a strange way I was part of a local legend.

It had rained heavily a few days before, and the path was muddy. I continued walking for some time, without a thought as to where I was guided. Suddenly the contours became familiar. I reached the open area into which I had run so many years ago, before being helped by strangers and before the ambulances and police cars arrived.

So many experiences separated the past and present that it felt as though that morning was part of another existence, long ago – yet in a strange way as though it were still only yesterday. As I looked towards the sky, all the experiences between these moments flashed before me, and in an instant I felt as though I had lived many lifetimes rolled into one and expressed countless personalities, yet remained essentially the same.

I continued walking along the path that I had followed only minutes after the attack. Stronger than ever before, I could feel my mother's presence all around me. Perhaps it was just the creator's energy assuring me that I was in the right place at the right time, doing what was right.

Soon I reached the spot where my mother had left her body. I knelt down on the soft earth. The minutes passed as I absorbed the comforting energy surrounding me.

I placed my hands together in prayer and closed my eyes.

'Thank you, Lord, for everything you've blessed me with. Thank you for making everything happen just the way it needs to happen. Thank you for making all the pieces of the puzzle come together in just the right way. Thank you, mother, for everything you gave me. I will always love you.'

EPILOGUE

'Molly, Molly!'

Suddenly I was brought back to the moment.

'Molly, Molly!' I heard someone calling again.

Was I dreaming? I stood up and turned around. Only metres away I spotted a man calling his dog.

I was certain. A higher power was watching over me, making sure that everything was perfect – and letting me know by sending a sign.

The light was beginning to fade. Soon it would be dark.

As I headed back towards the station with the sun sinking in the distance, my mind rushed back in time, and in the blink of an eye I saw my life's journey flash before me.

'What's next?' I wondered, as I contemplated the gift of life.

Each second we live is a new and unique moment of the universe, a moment that will never be again. And what do we teach our children? We teach them that two and two make four, and that Paris is the capital of France. When will we also teach them what they are? We should say to each of them: Do you know what you are? You are a marvel. You are unique. In all the years that have passed, there has never been another child like you. Your legs, your arms, your clever fingers, the way you move. You may become a Shakespeare, a Michelangelo, a Beethoven. You have the capacity for anything. Yes, you are a marvel. And when you grow up, can you then harm another who is, like you, a marvel? You must work, we must all work, to make the world worthy of its children.

Pau Casals

ACKNOWLEDGEMENTS

A big thank you to my father, to my agent Anna Power for her ongoing support and dedication, and to my editors Natalie Jerome and Kate Latham for their encouragement and belief in this project.